Global Economy Shifting Currents

Unveiling Global Economic Realities and Investment Frontiers

Bahaa G Arnouk

Global Economy Shifting Currents: Unveiling Global Economic Realities and Investment Frontiers

Book Cover by Bahaa Arnouk

1st edition 2024

Table of contents

Introduction 6

Chapter (1) United States: A Resilient Economic Powerhouse with Fresh Opportunities Amidst Fiscal Challenges 10

Chapter (2) China's High-Stakes Economic Evolution: Opportunities Amid Structural Risks and Policy Adjustments... 16

Chapter (3) Germany: A Resilient Economic Hub Facing Complex Challenges and Emerging Opportunities 24

Chapter (4) Japan: A Transformative Economic Landscape with Emerging Investment Horizons 31

Chapter (5) India's Economic Outlook: Resilience Amid Challenges and Strategic Reforms for Sustainable Growth......... 39

Chapter (6) United Kingdom: A Balanced Economic Recovery with Strategic Investment Opportunities Amidst Fiscal Pressures 48

Chapter (7) France: A Resilient Economy in Transition Amid Growing Fiscal Pressures and Green Ambitions 56

Chapter (8) Italy: A Resilient Economy with Strong Investment Potential Despite Structural Challenges.. 62

Chapter (9) Canada: A Resilient Economy Amid Housing and Fiscal Challenges, Poised for Green Growth 68

Chapter (10) Brazil: A Green and Digital Economy on the Rise 75

Chapter (11) South Korea's Economic Outlook: Navigating Growth, Debt, and Structural Challenges for a Sustainable Future.. 81

Chapter (12) Mexico: A Roadmap for Economic Resilience and Investment Amid Challenges 88

Global Economy Shifting Currents: Unveiling Global Economic Realities and Investment Frontiers

Chapter (13) Australia: Economic Resilience Amidst Challenges, with Focus on Productivity, Inflation Control, and Green Transformation 95

Chapter (14) Spain: A Recovering Economy with Growing Investment Potential Amid Challenges 102

Chapter (15) Indonesia's Economic Outlook: Growth, Debt, and the Road to High-Income Status... 109

Chapter (16) Turkey's Economic Outlook for 2025 and Beyond: Key Challenges and Growth Prospects... 116

Chapter (17) Netherlands: A Strategic Economic and Investment Landscape Amid Transition 123

Chapter (18) Saudi Arabia: A Thriving Economic Landscape Driving Global Investment Amid Transformation..................... 129

Chapter (19) Switzerland: Navigating Economic Resilience with Strategic Investments Amidst Fiscal and Demographic Challenges 136

Chapter (20) Argentina: A Blueprint for Economic Stability and Investment Amid Challenges 145

Chapter (21) The UAE's Financial System: A Rock of Stability in Uncertain Times.. 151

Chapter (22) Austria: A Strategic Economic and Investment Landscape Amidst Transition 157

Chapter (23) Singapore's Economic and Investment Landscape: Strategic Outlook for 2024 and Beyond..................................... 165

Chapter (24) Malaysia's Economic and Investment Landscape: In-Depth Strategic Outlook for future.. 174

Chapter (25) Navigating Egypt's Economic Transformation: Challenges, Opportunities, and a Glimpse of Hope 182

(Chapter 26) Iraq: Sensing the Potential: An Updated Look at Business Opportunities in Iraq... 187

Chapter (27) Greece: A Strategic Economic and Investment Landscape Amid Recovery and Structural Transformation 191

Chapter (28) Qatar: A Rising Star in the Gulf 200

Chapter (29) Kuwait: Navigating Economic Winds Amidst Abundant Wealth 205

Chapter (30) Oman: Embracing a Future Beyond Oil 210

Chapter (31) Jordan: A Beacon of Resilience in a Turbulent Region 217

Chapter (32) Cyprus: A Beacon of Resilience and Transformation in the Mediterranean 221

References 235

Introduction

In a rapidly changing global economy, the need for a clear, insightful understanding of economic shifts has never been greater. Across the world, markets are evolving in response to political decisions, technological advances, and the imperative for sustainable growth.

In **"Global Economy Shifting Currents"** Dr. Arnouk invites readers on a comprehensive journey through the economic landscapes of the world's most influential nations, exploring the forces shaping their futures and the emerging investment opportunities that lie within.

Each chapter of this book provides an exploration of a different nation's economic trajectory, from the powerhouse nations of North America and Europe to the emerging giants in Asia, Latin America, and the Middle East. The book addresses the complex interplay of economic recovery, fiscal strategies, labor market transformations, and technological innovations, while uncovering how each of these factors is redefining the investment climate. Key themes explored include:

Resilience and Recovery in Advanced Economies

Dr. Arnouk examines how countries like the United States and Germany are navigating fiscal challenges while seizing opportunities in digital transformation and green energy. The U.S., with its post-pandemic rebound, offers a wealth of opportunities in tech, healthcare, and green infrastructure. Meanwhile, Germany's green economy and manufacturing innovations stand as a beacon for investors focusing on long-term sustainability.

Economic Evolution in China and Japan

The book delves into China's high-stakes economic evolution, where shifting demographics, real estate crises, and digital innovation are at the core of its transformation. In parallel, Japan's blend of innovation and fiscal caution paves the way for opportunities in digitalization and sustainable energy solutions, particularly with its "Green Transformation" policies.

Emerging Economies with Untapped Potential

Countries like India, Brazil, and Indonesia are highlighted for their rapid growth and potential to reshape global trade dynamics. India's focus on infrastructure, digitalization, and green energy; Brazil's commitment to green finance and technological innovation; and Indonesia's path to high-income status are all prime examples of how emerging markets are positioning themselves as the next big players in the global economy.

Strategic Investment Horizons

Across these diverse landscapes, Dr. Arnouk provides invaluable insights into the sectors poised for the most significant growth—technology, green energy, infrastructure, and health. For instance, the green transition in the UAE, the rise of AI and cybersecurity in the U.S., and the innovative tech industries in Singapore offer investors a plethora of opportunities in high-growth, future-oriented sectors.

Geopolitical and Fiscal Challenges

The book doesn't shy away from addressing the fiscal constraints and geopolitical risks faced by many economies, from the U.K.'s fiscal pressures to the complex trade wars and debt crises impacting developing nations. Each chapter offers a nuanced perspective on how these challenges can be mitigated and how investors can leverage them to their advantage.

The Role of Sustainability in Shaping Global Growth

Dr. Arnouk discusses the critical role sustainability plays across all regions. From China's commitment to reducing carbon emissions to Europe's emphasis on green energy, sustainability isn't just a trend—it's shaping the future of investment. This book will show you where and how to invest in the green revolution that is transforming global industries.

In addition to the economic analyses, **"Global Economy Shifting Currents"** presents a roadmap for investors, policymakers, and business leaders to adapt to these evolving dynamics. Through strategic insights and country-specific perspectives,

With each chapter representing a global economic power or emerging economy, this book empowers you to understand the interconnectedness of world markets. Whether you are looking to diversify your portfolio, align with the green revolution, or gain a deeper understanding of the geopolitical landscape, **"Global Economy Shifting Currents"** is your essential guide to the future of the global economy.

Bahaa G. Arnouk

Chapter (1)

United States: A Resilient Economic Powerhouse with Fresh Opportunities Amidst Fiscal Challenges

The United States continues to impress with its post-pandemic rebound, defying expectations and maintaining robust demand, high employment, and strong growth prospects. The latest IMF report shows a vibrant economic landscape, rich with potential yet underscored by fiscal challenges that could shape the investment outlook. Here's a deep dive into the U.S. economic scene, where resilience meets risk and savvy investors are finding promising avenues for long-term gains.

A Dynamic Recovery: Economic Resilience Beyond the Headlines

The U.S. economic comeback is a case study in resilience. Even as global peers struggle with lingering post-pandemic effects, the U.S. economy has managed to exceed pre-pandemic employment and output levels. Key drivers of this remarkable recovery include:

Unmatched Consumer Demand: Bolstered by pandemic-era stimulus, household wealth surged, fueling a wave of spending. U.S. households benefited from a massive build-up in savings during the pandemic, combined with a 50% rise in housing prices. Real median net wealth has shot up by 34% since 2019, sustaining consumption across income groups and sectors.

Job Market Strength: The U.S. job market has not only bounced back but thrived, with 16 million new jobs since 2020. Labor force participation is at historic highs, thanks to an influx of skilled immigrant workers and higher wages that have drawn more workers into the fold. Unemployment is projected to remain at a healthy 4.2% in 2024

Taming Inflation: While inflationary pressures hit hard in 2022, peaking at 7.1%, the Federal Reserve's policy moves have stabilized inflation, which is expected to meet the Fed's 2% target by 2025. Aggressive rate hikes, improved productivity, and a stronger labor supply have combined to keep inflation under control, providing a stable foundation for investors.

This potent mix of growth drivers positions the U.S. as a robust global leader in economic stability and opportunity, even as fiscal concerns lurk.

Facing Fiscal Realities: The Challenge of Deficits and Debt

Beneath the U.S.'s dynamic economic surface lies a fiscal landscape that cannot be ignored. The U.S. is staring down unprecedented levels of public debt, with significant implications for long-term growth and market confidence.

Rising Deficits: The government deficit rose to 7.6% of GDP in 2023, with projections showing sustained levels unless structural changes are made. Public debt is on track to exceed 140% of GDP by 2032—a significant uptick driven by interest costs, healthcare spending, and demographic shifts

IMF's Call for Fiscal Realignment: The IMF is not mincing words: a substantial fiscal adjustment is necessary to stabilize debt trajectories and bolster confidence. The report suggests a series of targeted policy actions, from implementing a VAT and carbon tax to closing corporate loopholes. Progressive tax reforms and rebalancing social security and healthcare programs are among the recommended measures to reduce the deficit and ensure a sustainable future

Mitigating Fiscal Imbalance with Growth: The IMF underscores that a prudent fiscal adjustment, spread over time, could actually support U.S. growth, helping lower interest rates and enhancing market stability. This path, though challenging, would create a more reliable climate for long-term investment.

Investment Horizons: Growth Sectors with Promising Potential

Despite these fiscal headwinds, the U.S. remains a land of opportunity for investors looking to tap into cutting-edge industries and transformative growth areas. The IMF report shines a spotlight on high-growth sectors that align with America's policy priorities and long-term vision:

Digital Transformation and Tech: With a well-established lead in AI, cloud computing, and cybersecurity, the U.S. remains a global tech powerhouse. Driven by federal investment and private innovation, digital infrastructure is booming, making technology a safe harbor for investors seeking high-growth opportunities.

Green Energy and Infrastructure Renaissance: From the Inflation Reduction Act to the Infrastructure Investment and Jobs Act, green energy is taking center stage in America's growth story. Tax credits and subsidies for solar, wind, electric vehicles, and green grid technologies are flowing into the sector, creating robust investment opportunities in sustainable energy and infrastructure.

Healthcare and Biotech Advancements: With an aging population driving demand, healthcare is one of the U.S.'s highest growth sectors. Biotech innovation, telemedicine, and precision medicine are rapidly evolving, supported by strong domestic demand and technological advancements. Investment in these areas is increasingly attractive given the federal focus on healthcare affordability and access.

Manufacturing and Reshoring Initiatives: The U.S. government is investing billions to bring critical industries back home, spurred by the CHIPS Act and a growing focus on supply chain resilience. Semiconductor manufacturing and advanced manufacturing, especially in electric vehicles, are ripe for investment as the U.S. seeks to secure its supply chains and lead in high-value manufacturing.

These sectors not only promise growth but align with federal policies, offering long-term incentives and stability for investors who prioritize sustainability, innovation, and resilience.

Key Takeaways for Investors: Balancing Opportunity and Caution

The U.S. investment landscape offers a tantalizing array of opportunities, but it requires a nuanced approach. Fiscal concerns are real, but the potential for growth is equally compelling, particularly for those with an eye on strategic, policy-aligned investments. Here's how investors can position themselves:

Fiscal Vigilance Meets Market Optimism: Keep an eye on the fiscal climate and inflationary risks. Balancing a portfolio with inflation-resilient assets like tech and healthcare can help manage exposure to economic volatility.

Align with Federal Priorities for Stability: Government-backed sectors—such as green energy, digital transformation, and manufacturing—are poised for long-term growth. The Inflation Reduction Act, for example, promises stability and growth potential for renewables, making these sectors highly attractive.

Leverage ESG Trends for Long-Term Value: Environmental, social, and governance (ESG) criteria are growing in importance for U.S. businesses. Investors can gain an edge by focusing on sectors that meet ESG demands, including sustainable infrastructure and digital equity. Partnering with firms that prioritize ESG can enhance returns while tapping into growth aligned with U.S. priorities.

Think Long-Term with a Diverse Portfolio: The U.S. remains a beacon of innovation and economic strength, but diversification is essential. By investing across sectors like healthcare, technology, green energy, and manufacturing, investors can reduce risk and capture growth from multiple fronts.

The Future is Bright—For Those Ready to Act

While the U.S. faces real fiscal challenges, the country's core economic strengths, growth sectors, and policy-driven incentives make it an enticing market for investors with a forward-looking mindset. Navigating the U.S. landscape may require careful planning and strategic choices, but for those ready to act, the opportunities are rich and varied.

Are you prepared to harness the power of America's economic resilience? For investors ready to seize the moment, the U.S. economic landscape offers a powerful mix of stability, innovation, and sustainable growth.

Chapter (2)

China's High-Stakes Economic Evolution: Opportunities Amid Structural Risks and Policy Adjustments

China, as a global player, is navigating a transformative economic landscape marked by impressive growth, but with complex structural challenges. The IMF's latest insights on China's economy provide a nuanced picture: while recent policies have helped support growth, vulnerabilities, especially in the real estate sector and local government debt, present ongoing risks. For investors, understanding both the opportunities and the potential pitfalls in China's economic transition is essential to capitalizing on its evolving market. Below, we unpack the factors that make China's economy both promising and precarious.

Growth Against the Odds: Resilience in a Shifting Economy

China's post-pandemic recovery has showcased the resilience of its economy, despite substantial challenges. Supported by strong public investment and a consumption recovery, GDP expanded by 5.2% in 2023, and is expected to grow by 5% in 2024. However, the shadow of an ongoing real estate crisis looms, with property market contractions posing risks to broader economic stability.

Consumer Confidence Amid Structural Drag: A sharp post-pandemic rebound in private consumption, growing at 9% in 2023, has been vital for domestic demand. With consumer spending now stabilizing, China's economy is bolstered by a return to pre-pandemic saving rates. But as the property sector continues its painful correction, the impact on wealth, confidence, and local government revenue streams remains a question mark.

Low Inflation, High Stakes: Persistent disinflationary pressures, influenced by subdued domestic demand and low commodity prices, have kept inflation near zero. While the IMF expects consumer prices to rise modestly by 0.7% in 2024, core inflation remains subdued, suggesting ongoing economic slack that could affect medium-term growth.

Exports Stabilize as Services Grow: A declining current account surplus, which stood at 1.4% of GDP in 2023, highlights shifts in China's trade balance due to rising outbound tourism and global demand adjustments. While the export sector remains a pillar of China's economy, slower global growth and geopolitical pressures could constrain its future role.

Debt Dynamics and Fiscal Adjustments: Tackling Local Government Strains

China's fiscal strategy must balance support for growth with the heavy debt burdens weighing on local governments. The

IMF emphasizes that sustained fiscal reforms will be crucial to managing these pressures, particularly as property-related revenues decline.

Local Government Debt: The Hidden Risk: With a debt level equivalent to 124% of GDP, including local government financing vehicles (LGFVs), China's local government debt has reached precarious levels. A focus on supply-side initiatives like affordable housing and tax incentives for innovation places fiscal strain on local governments, particularly those heavily reliant on property-related revenues. The IMF suggests that further central government support and restructuring could be necessary to stabilize finances.

Easing Policy for Strategic Growth: In response to low inflation and economic slack, the People's Bank of China has been easing monetary policy through lower reserve requirements and interest rates, but local financial strains could complicate these efforts. The IMF advises continued easing, as well as exchange rate flexibility, to support demand and manage external pressures.

A New Fiscal Strategy: The 2024 budget reflects a balanced fiscal stance, with special bonds earmarked for strategic investments in digital and green technologies. This fiscal neutral approach, although cautious, highlights the government's intention to curb unsustainable debt accumulation while encouraging targeted growth.

The Green Horizon: China's Race to Lead in Renewable Energy and Innovation

Despite its fiscal and structural challenges, China's commitment to a green economy and technological innovation presents compelling growth opportunities. The IMF notes that China's investment in these areas, combined with a push to reduce carbon emissions, positions the country as a global leader in sustainable development.

Clean Energy and Emissions Reduction: China's green transformation is marked by significant investments in renewable energy and emissions trading. With its extensive use of emission permits and green infrastructure projects, China is making strides in reducing its carbon footprint, a positive signal for investors in green tech, renewable energy, and environmental technologies.

Innovation-Driven Economy: China's strategic pivot toward high-tech sectors, including AI, cloud computing, and next-generation manufacturing, supports growth in its digital economy. State-backed digital infrastructure initiatives make this sector a promising area for long-term investment. As China seeks to become a global leader in technology, opportunities abound in both hardware and software innovations.

Revitalizing Manufacturing: China's shift from low-value to high-value manufacturing offers a dynamic investment environment, especially as global supply chains evolve. For investors, opportunities in advanced manufacturing and export-oriented industries remain attractive, with the government's support reinforcing this trend.

Real Estate Reset: A Double-Edged Sword for Growth

China's real estate sector remains a point of vulnerability, with high unsold inventories, cash-strapped developers, and reluctant buyers casting a long shadow on the economy. The IMF underscores the importance of resolving real estate market imbalances to mitigate risks to financial stability and growth.

Housing Market Correction: Residential investment continues to decline, and the slump in new housing construction has not yet bottomed out. The IMF estimates that the completion of unfinished housing alone could cost around 5.5% of GDP over four years, with current policy adjustments potentially delaying resolution and increasing future fiscal costs.

High Developer Distress: Despite measures to support the housing market, solvency concerns remain widespread. About 50% of developers are facing severe financial difficulties, with an additional 15% struggling with liquidity. This distress exacerbates financial strains for both local governments and banks with significant exposure to the sector.

Balancing Risk and Demand: The government has introduced measures such as interest rate reductions and mortgage flexibility to stimulate demand, but further intervention, including allowing market-driven housing price adjustments, may be required to restore homebuyer confidence. The IMF suggests a comprehensive approach, including targeted fiscal resources and policies to address housing overhang and developer distress, is essential to stabilize the sector.

Navigating the Financial Landscape: Stability Amidst Elevated Risks

China's financial sector has shown resilience, yet vulnerabilities remain, especially among smaller banks and asset managers. The IMF warns of credit risks stemming from nonperforming loans in the property sector and mounting liabilities in local government financing vehicles.

Banking Sector Resilience: While major banks remain well-capitalized, smaller and rural banks face profitability and asset quality challenges, particularly those with high exposure to real estate. Regulatory reforms aimed at supporting smaller banks could provide stability, yet the IMF stresses the importance of crisis management frameworks to address systemic risks.

Corporate and Household Debt: With corporate debt at 122% of GDP and household debt around 60%, leveraging pressures are high. The IMF encourages measures to reduce debt accumulation, including fiscal support for struggling sectors and policies to stabilize the property market.

Financial System Reforms: As China's financial landscape evolves, strengthening risk oversight and transparency in the banking and asset management sectors will be critical. The IMF highlights the need for a coordinated strategy to reinforce smaller banks, strengthen crisis management, and manage potential spillovers from nonbank financial institutions.

Key Takeaways for Strategic Investment in China

For investors, China's economic landscape presents both high rewards and high risks. The country's focus on green growth, digital innovation, and structural reforms offers substantial opportunities, though caution is warranted due to fiscal and structural uncertainties.

Invest in Sustainability and High-Tech Innovation: China's ambitious environmental and technological goals, backed by substantial government support, make green and digital sectors particularly attractive.

Monitor Fiscal and Monetary Adjustments: China's balancing act between growth and debt reduction may impact sectors sensitive to fiscal policies and public investment. Staying attuned to these shifts is crucial.

Adopt a Diversified, Long-Term Strategy: Given China's structural transitions and policy shifts, a diversified approach across green energy, high-tech, and resilient manufacturing can capture growth while mitigating risks.

China's Path to High-Quality Growth: A Dual Challenge of Innovation and Reform

As China's economy transitions toward sustainability and innovation, a balanced approach is necessary to address its fiscal and structural challenges. While the potential for long-term growth remains strong, investors should be mindful of near-term risks in sectors like real estate and local government debt. With careful navigation, China offers a pathway for investors to engage in one of the world's most dynamic markets, where both resilience and reform are shaping the future.

Chapter (3)

Germany: A Resilient Economic Hub Facing Complex Challenges and Emerging Opportunities

Germany, the powerhouse of Europe, finds itself at a critical moment in its economic trajectory. While its reputation for industrial strength and stability remains, the country must navigate significant challenges, from the repercussions of the Russian-Ukrainian conflict to mounting competitive pressures from China. The latest IMF report reveals a nuanced picture of Germany's economic resilience, balanced against substantial demographic, fiscal, and geopolitical challenges. Here's an in-depth look at Germany's economic landscape, where cautious optimism meets potential hurdles, and where savvy investors might find unique opportunities amidst transformation.

A Steady Recovery: Strength and Resilience Amid Global Shifts

Germany's economy is on a path to recovery after weathering recent shocks, including soaring energy costs and global supply chain disruptions exacerbated by the Russian-Ukrainian conflict. Policy adjustments and Germany's robust industrial foundation have helped the country stabilize, with a gradual recovery on the horizon.

Consumer-Driven Growth Prospects: Despite previous economic setbacks, Germany's private consumption is projected to drive economic growth through 2024, as wages outpace inflation. With real wages turning positive, the IMF anticipates that GDP will grow by 0.2% in 2024 and 1.3% in 2025. Strong wage growth and stable consumption trends provide a promising climate for retail and service investments, even as fiscal and external pressures persist.

Energy Price Stabilization with Geopolitical Underpinnings: Germany's quick pivot away from Russian gas supplies has led to a stabilization of energy prices, reducing inflationary pressures that had previously stifled growth. After the shock of Russian supply disruptions, Germany diversified its energy sources, helping restore wholesale gas prices to manageable levels. The IMF notes that inflation is expected to ease, averaging 2.5% in 2024 and reaching 2.2% by 2025 ⌞OBJ⌟. This shift has major implications for energy-dependent sectors, which can now benefit from a more stable price environment.

Tight Labor Market with Slight Softening Ahead: Germany's unemployment rate, forecast to rise to 3.3% in 2024, reflects a still-tight labor market tempered by modest economic growth projections.

High wage growth has bolstered real household income, supporting consumption, but Germany's rapidly aging workforce signals potential long-term labor supply issues that could impact productivity without proactive policy adjustments in immigration and workforce integration. Germany's resilience in these areas highlights its role as a stable economic leader in Europe, but the economy remains exposed to significant risks, including heightened competition from China and the ongoing ramifications of the Russian-Ukrainian conflict, which has redefined Europe's geopolitical and energy landscape.

Fiscal Realities: Balancing Debt, Demographic Pressures, and Structural Reform

The IMF underscores substantial fiscal challenges facing Germany, particularly as demographic shifts and geopolitical demands place pressure on the government's fiscal capacity. Public spending is expected to increase significantly over the coming years, necessitating a balanced approach to fiscal reform and investment.

The Debt Brake and Calls for Fiscal Flexibility: Germany's debt brake, a constitutionally enshrined fiscal rule, has historically supported stability, but the IMF recommends considering moderate adjustments. A slight easing of this rule could free up fiscal space, enabling Germany to invest in infrastructure, digitalization, and green initiatives without risking debt sustainability. Adjusting the debt brake by about 1% of GDP could allow for the necessary public investment to support long-term growth.

Structural Reforms to Enhance Fiscal Capacity: To address growing fiscal needs, Germany is exploring a mix of revenue-enhancing and spending-reducing strategies. The IMF suggests that reforms such as eliminating environmentally harmful subsidies, increasing taxes on real estate, and closing tax loopholes could generate additional fiscal room, which is essential for meeting Germany's aging-related expenses, increased defence spending, and investment in green technologies. As Germany recalibrates its fiscal policies, it must balance these adjustments with the need for flexibility to respond to global uncertainties and demographic shifts. The recent shifts in energy policy and defence spending underscore Germany's responsiveness to geopolitical tensions, yet the fiscal burden from these commitments remains significant.

Investment Horizons: Promising Sectors Amid Transformative Shifts

Despite fiscal constraints, Germany's investment landscape is rich with sectors aligned with policy priorities and growth potential. The IMF report highlights key sectors positioned to thrive in Germany's economy, even as global competition and demographic changes shape the investment horizon.

Renewable Energy and Sustainability Initiatives: Germany's leadership in climate action has spurred investments in renewable energy. Following the challenges posed by the Russian-Ukrainian conflict, Germany accelerated its renewable energy initiatives, streamlining approval processes for wind and solar projects. For investors, these green sectors offer stability and alignment with Germany's climate goals, creating opportunities in sustainable energy infrastructure.

Technology and Digital Innovation: With an emphasis on reducing bureaucracy and expanding digital infrastructure, Germany is strengthening its digital economy. The government's investment in fibre optics, cloud computing, and AI presents a fertile ground for innovation and entrepreneurship. As competition from China intensifies, Germany's push to bolster digital capabilities serves as both a defence and an investment opportunity in the high-tech sector.

Healthcare and Aging Economy: With an aging population, Germany faces rising demand for healthcare services and eldercare. Investments in healthcare technology, biotech, and eldercare services are becoming increasingly attractive. These sectors are expected to grow alongside the country's demographic changes, driven by public demand and technological advancements that enhance service efficiency.

Manufacturing and Export Excellence in the Face of Global Competition: Germany's manufacturing sector, long a pillar of its economy, is shifting toward high-value products in response to intensifying global competition, particularly from China. The IMF notes that Germany's industrial sector is adapting to demand shifts by focusing on sectors with higher value-added potential, positioning itself favourably amidst changing trade dynamics. The export-oriented manufacturing industry offers investors a balance of stability and innovation, making it a reliable investment area even as global economic pressures rise. Strategic

Takeaways for Investors: Balancing Opportunity and Risk

Germany's investment landscape presents a mix of growth potential and fiscal caution, requiring a thoughtful investment approach. Here are some strategies for navigating Germany's economic landscape:

Align with Policy and ESG Priorities: The German government's focus on renewable energy, digital transformation, and healthcare aligns with EU policy priorities. Investors can leverage these sectors, which are likely to benefit from sustained government support and regulatory stability.

Sector-Specific Caution Amid Global Pressures: The IMF report highlights potential risks within Germany's real estate market, particularly commercial real estate (CRE), where prices have dropped due to high interest rates and changing market demands. Investors should be cautious about CRE exposure and consider sectors with stronger fundamentals, such as technology and healthcare

Sustainability and Long-Term Focus: ESG-focused investors can capitalize on Germany's strong commitment to sustainable practices. With established government support for green industries, Germany's sustainable sectors offer a long-term growth outlook that aligns with both environmental goals and regulatory frameworks.

Diverse Portfolios for Resilience: While Germany's market remains stable, the IMF warns that demographic pressures and geopolitical risks could impact growth. Diversifying across sectors—such as technology, renewable energy, healthcare, and high-value manufacturing—can help mitigate these risks, enabling investors to capture growth while managing volatility.

Germany's Future Path: Resilience in an Evolving Global Landscape

Germany's economic outlook remains robust, underpinned by strategic sectors that align with global priorities. However, fiscal challenges, demographic shifts, and heightened competition—particularly from China—add complexity to the nation's growth trajectory. Investors with a long-term, balanced approach can find ample opportunities in Germany's diverse economic landscape, but success will require navigating the nuanced risks posed by fiscal pressures, global competition, and the ongoing impacts of the Russian Ukrainian conflict. For those prepared to invest with a strategic vision, Germany offers a blend of stability, innovation, and sustainable growth.

Chapter (4)

Japan: A Transformative Economic Landscape with Emerging Investment Horizons

Japan's economy is undergoing a carefully calibrated recovery, blending strategic fiscal stimulus with policy innovations to address long-standing structural challenges. This blend of resilience and foresight positions Japan as a unique investment environment, rich with opportunities in digital (DX) and green transformations (GX), albeit marked by fiscal sustainability challenges and demographic pressures. The IMF's 2024 report on Japan highlights these dynamics, offering insights for investors poised to capitalize on Japan's evolving economic path.

Resilient Economic Recovery and Inflation Dynamics

Japan's economy has rebounded gradually since the pandemic, with GDP now above pre-pandemic levels, bolstered by exports and a revived tourism sector. Key growth drivers include:

Stable Inflation Trajectory: Japan has achieved a sustained period of above-target inflation for the first time in decades.

Headline inflation, though expected to ease, will likely remain above the 2% target until mid-2025, due to robust wage increases and ongoing demand recovery.

Strength in Consumption: Despite some headwinds in real wage growth, the ongoing Shunto wage negotiations have delivered notable wage hikes, with an anticipated uptick in real consumption toward the latter half of 2024. These dynamics underscore Japan's unique inflation landscape and highlight emerging demand potential.

Fiscal Policies: Balancing Transformation with Debt Management

Japan's fiscal landscape features transformative policies aimed at revitalizing key sectors, but this is accompanied by heightened debt levels and a critical need for fiscal discipline. The IMF underscores:

Debt Challenges: Japan's public debt-to-GDP ratio, standing at over 250%, requires cautious management. Fiscal consolidation is essential to counterbalance the expansive policy measures and ensure long-term fiscal sustainability. The IMF recommends a trajectory that involves broadening the tax base, optimizing healthcare expenditures, and aligning fiscal stimulus with targeted growth policies.

Strategic Fiscal Reforms: The IMF advocates for structural reforms, emphasizing progressive taxation, healthcare cost controls, and targeted social spending. These fiscal measures will be crucial to managing the pressures from an aging population and sustaining growth momentum.

Bahaa G. Arnouk

Digital Transformation (DX) Initiatives: Japan's Path to a Digital Economy

Japan's digital transformation (DX) ambitions are central to its "new capitalism" agenda, targeting innovations across AI, digital infrastructure, and technological modernization:

National Digital Infrastructure: Under its DX strategy, Japan is significantly investing in digital infrastructure to modernize its economy. Key initiatives include expanding 5G networks, AI development, and enhancing cybersecurity frameworks. These projects are supported by government subsidies and partnerships with private enterprises, aiming to streamline digital governance and position Japan as a leader in digital innovation.

AI and Automation Investment: AI and automation are cornerstones of Japan's DX initiative, with a focus on boosting productivity in industries like manufacturing, healthcare, and logistics. The government has earmarked significant funds to support AI-driven projects, alongside public-private partnerships to foster innovation in sectors facing labor shortages.

Future Trajectory and Impact: DX is expected to drive Japan's productivity and economic growth by addressing labor market shortages and enhancing competitiveness. Japan's trajectory in DX projects is poised to attract investment across sectors, as these digital initiatives are tightly integrated with its broader economic transformation plans.

Green Transformation (GX): Leading Japan to a Sustainable Future

Japan's green transformation (GX) strategy is a comprehensive approach to achieving carbon neutrality and fostering sustainable development. The GX initiatives target energy efficiency, renewable energy, and infrastructure resilience:

Renewable Energy Expansion: GX projects are significantly advancing Japan's energy landscape. The government has laid out substantial subsidies for solar, wind, and hydrogen energy sectors, aligned with the goal of reducing carbon emissions by 46% by 2030 and achieving carbon neutrality by 2050. These subsidies and tax incentives are designed to attract private sector investments and scale up renewable energy capacity.

Infrastructure and Resilience Projects: Beyond renewable energy, Japan's GX agenda encompasses infrastructure resilience, such as reinforcing disaster preparedness and sustainable urban development. This includes green building standards, enhanced public transit systems, and eco-friendly technology in housing. The focus on resilient infrastructure aims to mitigate risks associated with climate change while promoting sustainable urbanization.

Green Technology and Export Opportunities: GX investments also extend to green technology exports, enabling Japan to capitalize on its innovation in areas such as electric vehicle (EV) technology and battery manufacturing. As Japan strengthens its green tech export capabilities, it is expected to become a regional leader in sustainable technology, offering investment prospects within and beyond its borders.

Financial Sector Resilience and Real Estate Oversight

Japan's financial sector has maintained stability despite global uncertainties, bolstered by resilient banking capital and liquidity frameworks, but select vulnerabilities remain:

Strength in Banking and Insurer Portfolios: Japanese banks are well-capitalized with robust liquidity, and non-performing loans are at record lows. However, banks with substantial foreign currency exposure face risks from exchange rate volatility, warranting continuous monitoring. Insurers, another robust sector, have also adapted their portfolios amid rising hedging costs, showcasing Japan's financial resilience.

Real Estate Sector Oversight: Japan's commercial real estate (CRE) market, particularly in urban areas, has seen strong growth, but the IMF has highlighted the need for proactive risk management in the event of potential real estate price corrections. Macroprudential policies, including monitoring loan exposure and borrower resilience, will be vital for sustained stability.

Key Sectors for Investment: Growth Potential in DX, GX, and Healthcare

Japan's economy, while facing demographic and fiscal constraints, offers attractive investment opportunities in key sectors supported by government initiatives:

Digital Innovation and DX: As Japan accelerates its digital transformation, investments in AI, 5G, cybersecurity, and automation are highly attractive. The government's DX policies are setting the stage for long-term growth in these sectors, making them vital areas for investors focused on technology and productivity.

Green Energy and GX Projects: The green transformation initiatives create substantial opportunities in renewable energy, eco-infrastructure, and green technology exports. GX investments are heavily incentivized through subsidies and tax breaks, aligning well with Japan's sustainability goals and creating a favorable environment for investors in clean tech and infrastructure resilience.

Healthcare and Aging Solutions: With one of the world's oldest populations, Japan's healthcare sector is ripe for investment, particularly in biotech, elderly care technology, and telemedicine. Innovations in this space are supported by Japan's policies targeting healthcare modernization and accessibility.

Strategic Investment Takeaways: Balancing Transformation with Prudence

Investors looking to capitalize on Japan's dynamic economic landscape should consider a balanced approach, weighing growth potential against fiscal and demographic headwinds. Strategic takeaways include:

Target Policy-Aligned Sectors: Sectors prioritized by the Japanese government, such as digital innovation (DX), green transformation (GX), and healthcare, are not only growth-oriented but benefit from policy support, providing stability amid fiscal challenges.

Long-Term Resilience with Diverse Portfolios: Japan's economic policies, particularly in GX and DX, offer sustained growth potential, making a diversified investment approach across these sectors beneficial. Additionally, these investments align with global Environmental, Social, and Governance (ESG) trends, which are increasingly significant for value-driven investors.

Fiscal Awareness in Investment Strategy: Despite promising growth sectors, Japan's high public debt and aging demographic necessitate cautious fiscal monitoring. Investments in inflation-resilient sectors such as technology, healthcare, and green energy can help mitigate economic volatility risks for investors.

Japan's Economic Horizon: A New Era of Innovation and Sustainability

Japan's economic landscape reflects a nuanced recovery marked by innovation-led initiatives in digital and green transformations. The IMF report underscores Japan's commitment to a sustainable, technologically advanced future, setting the foundation for resilient growth. For investors with a long-term perspective, Japan offers a compelling blend of stability, growth, and sectoral opportunities in line with the global shift toward sustainable development.

Are you ready to navigate Japan's transformative economic path? Japan's blend of policy-driven growth, coupled with its commitment to sustainability and technological advancement, provides a strategic foundation for forward-looking investors.

Chapter (5)

India's Economic Outlook: Resilience Amid Challenges and Strategic Reforms for Sustainable Growth

India is firmly positioned as one of the world's most dynamic and rapidly growing economies. As one of the fastest-growing major economies globally, India has emerged as a key driver of global economic momentum, despite facing a range of domestic and international challenges. According to the IMF's latest *Article IV Consultation* report, India's economy has demonstrated strong recovery and resilience post-pandemic, buoyed by robust domestic demand, public investment, and an expanding service sector. However, the country continues to grapple with rising public debt, inflationary pressures, fiscal deficits, and external vulnerabilities. As the country steers through these economic complexities, it presents both substantial opportunities and risks for investors. Below, we take a deeper dive into India's current economic landscape, drawing insights from the IMF's findings for FY2023/24 and the medium-term trajectory.

India's Robust Growth Story: Powered by Consumption and Public Investment

India's economy is projected to grow at 6.3% in both FY2023/24 and FY2024/25, supported by strong domestic demand and resilient service exports. In FY2022/23, real GDP growth reached 7.2%, a moderation from 9.1% in FY2021/22 but still showcasing India's strong recovery post-pandemic. The IMF attributes this growth to a combination of factors including pent-up demand from households, strong public sector capital expenditure, and a surge in outsourcing-related services exports driven by the global recovery from COVID-19. Although global economic growth has slowed, India's domestic factors—particularly infrastructure investment and consumption recovery—are expected to ensure stable growth.

India's continued emphasis on infrastructure investment is critical to sustaining growth. The government's capital expenditure plans have been a cornerstone of fiscal policy, aiming to crowd in private sector investment by addressing the country's infrastructure gaps, particularly in energy, transportation, and urban development. Public investments are expected to continue to fuel demand in these areas, while fostering a conducive environment for private sector participation, particularly through public-private partnerships (PPPs).

While the pent-up consumption from the pandemic is starting to moderate, the rise in domestic private sector investment is expected to sustain growth. Additionally, the government's focus on expanding the digital economy, including innovations in digital infrastructure, holds significant promise for further productivity gains and economic expansion.

Inflation: Managing Volatility Amid Structural Shocks

Inflation has been a persistent issue for India, with headline inflation reaching as high as 7.4% in July 2023, driven by volatility in food prices, especially vegetables. This uptick was primarily a result of weather-related supply shocks, including a 202% year-on-year increase in tomato prices. However, inflationary pressures began to moderate in August 2023, with CPI inflation falling back within the RBI's target band of 4±2% by September.

The IMF expects inflation to gradually decline, reaching 5.4% in FY2023/24 before converging toward the 4% target over the medium term. Core inflation, which excludes food and fuel items, has also seen moderation, falling to 4.5% by September 2023, reflecting the RBI's effective monetary policy tightening and the easing of global commodity prices.

However, the volatility in food prices remains a concern. India's inflation dynamics are unique due to the substantial weight of food prices in its CPI basket, which accounts for a large portion of household consumption. The IMF report notes that food price shocks—whether from adverse weather events or global supply chain disruptions—pose a significant risk to India's inflation trajectory. As a result, the Reserve Bank of India (RBI) has maintained a vigilant stance, implementing monetary tightening to bring inflation under control, but risks from exogenous shocks continue to loom.

Fiscal Policy: Debt Sustainability and Medium-Term Challenges

India's fiscal landscape is under considerable strain. The IMF's report highlights that while the fiscal deficit has improved from the pandemic highs, it remains elevated at 6.5% of GDP in FY2022/23, with projections indicating a slight reduction to 6.0% in FY2023/24. Despite a narrowing of the budget deficit, India's public debt remains high, expected to reach 82% of GDP in FY2023/24.

India's fiscal strategy aims to balance supporting growth with fiscal consolidation. Public debt sustainability is a key challenge, and the IMF advises that ambitious medium-term fiscal consolidation efforts are needed to lower debt levels and rebuild fiscal buffers. This will require enhancing revenue mobilization through tax reforms, particularly focusing on improving compliance and expanding the tax base. The implementation of digitalization initiatives aimed at streamlining tax administration, including the Goods and Services Tax (GST) system, is seen as crucial for improving tax revenue.

The IMF also recommends that India improve the efficiency of public spending by targeting subsidies more effectively, especially in sectors such as food and fuel. The government's efforts to streamline subsidies and direct transfers using digital identification systems could reduce fiscal costs and improve the effectiveness of social support.

Debt Dynamics: Sovereign Risks and the Need for Fiscal Reforms

While India's debt is largely composed of long-term, fixed-rate instruments in local currency, the sheer volume of debt presents significant challenges. The government's fiscal deficit is expected to gradually decline, but the debt-to-GDP ratio is anticipated to remain high, peaking at 82% in FY2024/25 before starting a downward trajectory. The IMF's baseline scenario anticipates that India will continue to face substantial gross financing needs, with public debt as a percentage of GDP expected to remain high in the medium term.

India's relatively low external debt—around 18% of GDP—provides some insulation from external financial shocks, but the country still faces significant vulnerabilities. The IMF underscores the importance of continuing with fiscal consolidation while focusing on targeted public investment in infrastructure and social support. However, structural reforms in the public financial management system are essential to mitigate risks related to contingent liabilities from the electricity distribution sector, which has historically required substantial state intervention.

External Sector: Strengthening Resilience Amid Global Volatility

India's external sector has shown improvement, with foreign exchange reserves recovering from the pressures of global financial volatility in 2022. By mid-2023, India's reserves stood at approximately US$587 billion, enough to cover more than seven months of prospective imports. This provides a strong buffer against external shocks, particularly from geopolitical tensions or commodity price volatility.

The current account deficit (CAD) has widened to 2% of GDP in FY2022/23, mainly due to higher commodity imports and a recovery in domestic demand. However, the IMF forecasts a narrowing of the CAD to 1.8% of GDP in FY2023/24, supported by resilient services exports and reduced oil import costs as India diversifies its energy sources, including the significant increase in discounted Russian oil imports.

Despite these positive developments, external risks remain significant. The global growth slowdown and supply chain disruptions could impact India's trade balance, especially as it faces the challenges of rising import costs. Additionally, geopolitical risks, such as global commodity price fluctuations and supply disruptions, could create further volatility in India's external sector.

Financial Sector Resilience: Managing Risk in a Growing Market

India's financial sector has remained resilient, with the banking system showing improved capital buffers and reduced non-performing assets (NPAs). The IMF reports that the capital-to-risk-weighted assets ratio reached a record high of 17.2% in March 2023, and bank profitability has improved significantly. Non-performing asset ratios are at multiyear lows, contributing to a more stable financial system.

However, challenges remain, particularly with smaller non-bank financial companies (NBFCs) and urban cooperative banks (UCBs), which remain vulnerable to liquidity and credit risks. The rapid growth in personal loans has also raised concerns about future financial stress, requiring careful monitoring by the RBI.

The IMF emphasizes the need for continued vigilance in banking sector supervision, with the use of prudential tools to mitigate emerging risks. Strengthening the governance of public banks and expanding access to credit for small and medium enterprises (SMEs) will be crucial to maintaining financial sector stability.

Structural Reforms: Key to Unlocking India's Potential for Inclusive Growth

India's demographic advantage—its large, young population—presents immense potential for growth, but only if accompanied by comprehensive structural reforms. The IMF stresses that India's growth potential could be significantly enhanced by reforms in areas such as labor markets, agriculture, education, and healthcare. Key to these reforms is increasing female labor force participation and improving the quality of jobs in the formal sector.

The digital revolution, driven by the government's emphasis on public digital infrastructure, is also expected to provide substantial gains in productivity and efficiency across the economy.

India's ambitious green transition, including its focus on renewable energy, offers significant opportunities for investment in the environmental and clean energy sectors. With the government committed to its net-zero emissions target, investments in green technologies and sustainability are poised to grow, further enhancing India's role in global climate leadership.

Key Takeaways for Investors:

Invest in Infrastructure and Green Growth: India's continued investment in infrastructure and renewable energy provides long-term opportunities.

Monitor Fiscal and Debt Dynamics: Pay attention to India's fiscal consolidation efforts and public debt management, which could affect investment in government securities and related sectors.

Leverage Digital Innovation: India's digital economy presents significant growth potential, driven by government-backed digital infrastructure initiatives.

Diversify to Mitigate Risks: Stay attuned to inflation volatility, external trade risks, and fiscal pressures to strategically diversify investments.

Conclusion: A Path of Resilience and Opportunity

India's economic trajectory is characterized by strong growth, rising public debt, and the need for fiscal and structural reforms. For investors, India offers significant opportunities, particularly in infrastructure, green energy, and digital sectors. However, the risks—particularly related to fiscal sustainability, inflation, and external vulnerabilities—require careful navigation.

India's economic potential remains robust, but realizing this potential will require continued fiscal discipline, effective management of public debt, and comprehensive structural reforms to drive inclusive, sustainable growth. With strategic investments and careful risk management, India offers a promising outlook for the long term, as it continues to play a crucial role in shaping the global economic future.

India's future will be shaped by its ability to balance growth with fiscal prudence, all while embracing innovation and reform to unlock the full potential of its economy.

Chapter (6)

United Kingdom: A Balanced Economic Recovery with Strategic Investment Opportunities Amidst Fiscal Pressures

As the United Kingdom moves through a period of economic recalibration, the latest IMF report on the country's 2024 economic outlook provides a nuanced view of both the challenges and opportunities ahead. The UK is on a path of recovery after a mild recession in 2023, and while inflation is subsiding and growth prospects are improving, the fiscal landscape remains burdened by significant spending pressures, particularly in healthcare and public services. For investors, this presents a mixed bag of risks and rewards, with key areas for growth emerging in response to government policies and structural reforms. This detailed analysis takes a deep dive into the UK's economic and investment landscape, highlighting the numbers, projections, and policy measures shaping the country's future.

Bahaa G. Arnouk

A Soft Economic Landing with Signs of Recovery

Despite a mild technical recession in 2023, the UK economy is on a path to recovery, with growth expected to rise from 0.1% in 2023 to 0.7% in 2024 and 1.5% in 2025. This moderate rebound is largely driven by the stabilization of inflation and the easing of financial conditions, supported by the Bank of England's (BoE) cautious approach to monetary policy.

Key Factors Behind the Recovery:

Inflation Easing Rapidly: The inflationary pressures that plagued the UK in 2022, where inflation peaked at 7.3%, have started to ease significantly. By 2024, inflation is projected to fall to 2.7% annually, with expectations to drop further to 2% by 2025. This disinflationary trend is mainly attributed to lower energy prices and the tightening effects of previous monetary policies. However, wage and services inflation remain persistent at elevated levels, with wage growth projected at 5.7% in April 2024, which could dampen real income growth in the short term.

Monetary Policy Adjustments: The BoE has recently moved toward a more neutral stance, pausing interest rate hikes in favor of assessing economic conditions. The bank's approach is likely to include a series of rate cuts beginning in the latter half of 2024, as inflation expectations begin to moderate and as the economy transitions from restrictive to more accommodative monetary conditions. This shift in monetary policy provides a much-needed cushion for businesses and consumers burdened by high borrowing costs over the last year.

Private Consumption and Business Investment Recovery: Despite the initial setback in 2023, consumer spending is expected to pick up in 2024, though it remains sluggish compared to pre-pandemic levels. On the investment side, the government's fiscal policy, including tax cuts and incentives aimed at improving the labor supply, is providing some momentum for business growth, particularly in areas aligned with public sector goals such as the green transition and technology sectors.

While the economic recovery appears on track, the UK's fiscal landscape remains constrained by long-term structural challenges. The IMF's report highlights several pressing fiscal issues that could limit the UK's ability to achieve sustained growth without major reforms:

Fiscal Deficits and Debt Trajectory:

Public Debt and Deficits: The UK's fiscal deficit reached 4.2% of GDP in 2023, and while it is projected to improve modestly, the public sector net debt (excluding the Bank of England) is expected to rise from 89.2% of GDP in 2023 to 94.5% by 2026. This indicates that while the government has made progress in controlling the deficit, it faces an uphill battle in stabilizing public debt without further fiscal consolidation or significant boosts to economic growth.

Rising Public Service Costs: Spending on public services, especially healthcare and social care, is escalating due to an aging population and rising demand for services. The IMF estimates that these pressures, combined with the effects of long-term illness and increasing disability rates, will require substantial investment to avoid a strain on government resources. To meet these requirements, the UK will need to implement bold fiscal measures, including tax reforms and cuts to inefficient subsidies.

The Need for Structural Reforms: The IMF emphasizes that without substantial growth-enhancing reforms, the UK faces limited medium-term growth prospects. Factors such as weak labor productivity, a declining workforce due to population aging, and the adverse effects of Brexit continue to drag on economic performance. Addressing these challenges will require major investments in skills development, technology, and healthcare.

Taxation and Fisca:

Revenues and Tax Reforms: The IMF highlights several potential revenue-raising measures to help stabilize the fiscal outlook, including aligning capital gains tax rates with income tax, removing unnecessary VAT exemptions, and reforming property taxation. These changes could help diversify the base and reduce the fiscal deficit, while promoting fairness and efficiency in the tax system.

Spending Efficiency and Investment: On the spending side, the government must address its inefficiencies, particularly in the NHS and social care sectors. The IMF recommends that funds be directed toward health workforce investments and digital infrastructure, which would improve service delivery while easing long-term pressures. Furthermore, the government should continuities high-value investments in the green transition, which will not only foster sustainable growth but also contribute to long-term fiscal stability.

Growth Opportunities Amidst the Fiscal Pressures

Despite the fiscal constraints, the UK economy presents several growth sectors that investors can tap into, particularly those that align with government priorities and structural reforms. These areas not only offer robust growth potential but also come with policy-driven incentives that could provide stability for long-term investors.

Key Investment Sectors:

Green Energy and Infrastructure: The UK government is committed to reducing carbon emissions and transitioning to a low-carbon economy. This includes significant investments in renewable energy, electric vehicles, and green infrastructure. The IMF underscores the importance of a stable fiscal framework to support these efforts, suggesting that stronger carbon taxes and green investment incentives will drive future growth in this sector. For investors, the green transition offers opportunities for capital growth, especially in companies that are positioned as leaders in clean technology.

Technology and Artificial Intelligence: As the UK seeks to enhance labor productivity and economic competitiveness, the adoption of new technologies, particularly artificial intelligence (AI), will play a critical role. The IMF report suggests that significant upside potential exists in AI and other digital transformation initiatives, especially as the government focuses on developing a more skilled workforce. The country's strong tech ecosystem, supported by digital infrastructure and skills development, presents a ripe opportunity for investors in technology sectors, especially AI-driven solutions in healthcare, finance, and manufacturing.

Healthcare and Life Sciences: Given the aging population and increasing healthcare demands, biotech, life sciences, and health-related investments are expected to see robust growth. The UK's commitment to reforming its healthcare system, along with investments in the NHS workforce, positions the sector for long-term development. Investors in healthcare innovation, particularly in biotechnology and telemedicine, should find promising avenues as the government continues to focus on improving healthcare delivery.

Real Estate and Commercial Property: Despite high interest rates, the UK's real estate market has shown resilience. House prices are projected to remain stable, and the commercial real estate sector is beginning to recover from its 2022 downturn. The IMF notes that the market is likely to avoid a major correction, with demand continuing in key regions like London and Northern Ireland. For investors in real estate, the outlook remains positive, opportunities in both residential and commercial properties.

Key Takeaways for Investors

As the UK navigates its economic recovery, investors must balance the potential for growth with the fiscal challenges ahead. Here are key insights for making strategic investment decisions:

Stay Ahead of Fiscal Policy Shifts: Watch for changes in the government's fiscal policy, especially related to tax reforms and public spending adjustments. Sectors that align with these reforms, such as green energy and healthcare, will benefit from government support.

Focus on High-Growth Sectors: Despite the fiscal challenges, sectors like green energy, technology, and healthcare are well-positioned for long-term growth. Capitalizing on these opportunities will require a keen understanding of the government's investment priorities.

Invest in Innovation and Productivity: AI and digital transformation are poised to be major drivers of UK productivity in the coming years. For investors, this means focusing on companies and technologies that leverage these innovations.

Diversify in Resilient Sectors: While the real estate market faces short-term challenges, certain areas, particularly residential properties in high-demand regions, continue to offer strong investment opportunities. Commercial real estate, too, is showing signs of recovery and could benefit from ongoing economic adjustments.

Conclusion: A Path to Sustainable Growth

The United Kingdom faces a complex yet promising economic landscape. While fiscal challenges remain, the country's recovery trajectory is supported by easing inflation, targeted fiscal measures, and strategic investments in high-growth sectors. For investors, the key will be to align with government priorities in green energy, technology, and healthcare, while being mindful of the fiscal constraints that could shape long-term growth. With a focus on innovation, sustainability, and strategic reforms, the UK's economic future holds significant potential for those willing to navigate its evolving landscape.

Chapter (7)

France: A Resilient Economy in Transition Amid Growing Fiscal Pressures and Green Ambitions

As the second-largest economy in the Eurozone, France faces a complex economic landscape shaped by recent global shocks and its ambitious green and digital transformation agendas. While its economic recovery has shown signs of resilience, the country grapples with fiscal pressures, an aging population, and geopolitical challenges. The latest IMF consultation report offers valuable insights into France's economic outlook, detailing its ongoing recovery, fiscal consolidation efforts, and the significant opportunities for growth in critical sectors. Below is an in-depth exploration of France's economic environment, highlighting key trends and areas where investors may find promising opportunities.

Economic Recovery: Gradual Growth Amidst Global Challenges

France's economy has displayed resilience in the face of multiple shocks, including the COVID-19 pandemic and the energy crisis triggered by the Russian invasion of Ukraine.

Despite a slowdown in 2023, GDP grew by 1.1%, supported by net exports, especially in aeronautics and textiles. However, domestic demand remained weak, and investment, particularly in residential construction, surprised on the downside.

Moderate Growth in 2024: France's economy is projected to grow by 0.9% in 2024, driven by recovery in exports and a gradual pickup in investment. While inflation pressures have eased significantly since 2023, the path to a full recovery remains uncertain, with global factors, such as geopolitical tensions and a potential slowdown in major trading partners, influencing the outlook.

Disinflationary Progress: Inflation, which peaked at 7.3% in early 2023, is on track to fall to 2.3% by the end of 2024, thanks to easing energy prices and improved supply chain conditions. Core inflation, which excludes volatile food and energy prices, is also declining, albeit at a slower pace, highlighting ongoing challenges in the services sector.

Labor Market Strength: France's labor market remains robust, with low unemployment rates around 7.4% in 2024, despite weaker economic conditions. However, labor productivity has yet to recover fully from the pandemic-induced disruptions, and structural reforms in the pension and unemployment systems are expected to support longer-term job growth and productivity improvement.

Fiscal Strategy: Navigating High Debt and Demographic Pressures

The IMF report highlights the importance of fiscal consolidation as France seeks to reduce its public debt and meet rising demands for investment in green and digital initiatives. The fiscal deficit reached 5.5% of GDP in 2023, driven by underperformance in tax revenues and higher-than-expected spending. The 2024 budget aims to reduce the deficit to 5.1%, but the road to fiscal sustainability is steep.

Pension and Unemployment Benefit Reforms: Reforms to the pension system and unemployment benefits are beginning to show positive results, but further efforts are required to bring the deficit below 3% of GDP by 2027. These reforms aim to reduce structural unemployment and raise potential output, providing some relief to public finances.

Public Debt Concerns: With public debt at 111.3% of GDP in 2024, France faces significant challenges in managing its fiscal trajectory. The government's commitment to reducing the deficit through targeted spending cuts and new revenue-generating measures is crucial. While the IMF forecasts moderate fiscal improvements over the medium term, debt sustainability remains a key concern.

Tax and Spending Reforms: The IMF suggests a focus on reducing inefficiencies in public spending, particularly in sectors like health, education, and social security. The French authorities have already initiated spending reviews and aim to streamline expenditures while protecting investments in green energy and digital infrastructure.

Investment Horizons: Green Transition, Digital Innovation, and More

Despite fiscal constraints, France's transformation towards a greener and more digital economy presents significant investment opportunities.

Green Economy and Renewable Energy: France's green transition is at the heart of its economic future. The country is committed to reducing greenhouse gas emissions and has allocated significant resources to sustainable projects, such as building renovations, public transport, and low-emission vehicles. This focus on environmental sustainability offers growth potential in green technologies, renewable energy, and infrastructure development.

Digital Transformation: France is also positioning itself as a leader in digital innovation. Investments in digital infrastructure, including fibre optics, AI, and cloud computing, are driving growth in the tech sector. The government's efforts to enhance digital capabilities present investment opportunities, particularly as the global economy shifts toward digitalization.

Manufacturing and Export Growth: The manufacturing sector, particularly aeronautics and automotive, continues to be a cornerstone of the French economy. With exports expected to recover, these industries present a stable yet dynamic investment landscape, especially as France adapts to new global trade patterns.

Risks and Opportunities: Balancing Economic Challenges with Growth Potential

While France's economic outlook is positive, the road ahead is fraught with risks, particularly in the areas of fiscal sustainability, demographic shifts, and geopolitical tensions.

Political Fragmentation and Fiscal Uncertainty: Domestic political fragmentation and policy uncertainty could delay necessary fiscal reforms, affecting investor confidence and economic growth. The outcome of France's 2024 legislative elections with a New Popular Front (NFP) in the lower house of parliament, a left-wing alliance that won 182 seats, a centrist coalition with only 168 seats and a hard-wing party that won only 143 seats, the NFP is short of majority and the country has got a hung parliament that is shaping the country's fiscal and economic trajectory.

Geopolitical and Global Economic Risks: The ongoing geopolitical instability in Europe, compounded by a potential slowdown in global growth, could dampen France's external demand. Investors must remain cautious of these external risks, especially in sectors reliant on global trade.

Strategic Takeaways for Investors:

Focus on Green and Digital Sectors: With strong government backing, sectors related to renewable energy, digital infrastructure, and sustainable technologies offer long-term growth potential.

Monitor Fiscal Developments: France's ongoing fiscal adjustments provide opportunities in sectors that align with government priorities, but caution is warranted in industries sensitive to tax increases or public spending cuts.

Diversify Investments: Given France's fiscal and geopolitical uncertainties, a diversified investment strategy across sectors like technology, healthcare, and manufacturing will help mitigate risks while capturing growth opportunities.

A Balanced Path Forward for France's Economic Transformation

France stands at a crossroads, balancing the need for fiscal prudence with its ambitions for a green and digital future. As the country continues to recover from recent shocks, the strategic focus on green energy, digital innovation, and structural reforms presents a wealth of opportunities for forward-thinking investors. However, the fiscal challenges and global uncertainties underscore the need for a measured, diversified investment approach to navigate France's evolving economic landscape.

Chapter (8)

Italy: A Resilient Economy with Strong Investment Potential Despite Structural Challenges

Italy's economic outlook in 2024 is marked by cautious optimism, underscored by a recovery from the COVID-19 and energy price shocks. While growth in 202 3 was moderate at 0.9%, Italy's economy is projected to stabilize with gradual improvements. Despite challenges such as weak productivity, an aging population, and ongoing fiscal pressures, Italy presents an investment environment rich with opportunities—especially in the green and digital transitions, infrastructure development, and private sector innovation. The IMF's recent consultation report highlights Italy's strengths and risks, offering a roadmap for future growth and investment.

Economic Outlook: Growth Moderates but Resilience Remains

Italy's real GDP grew by 0.9% in 2023, surpassing pre-pandemic levels for the first time in 15 years. While growth is forecast to slow in the coming years, stabilizing at around 0.7% in 2024, the economic recovery remains solid compared to other Eurozone economies. Growth has been supported by private consumption and investment, notably fueled by tax credits for home renovations and capital equipment purchases. However, Italy faces long-term challenges from a shrinking workforce and low productivity growth.

Private Consumption and Investment: Despite a boost from tax credits and public investment under the National Recovery and Resilience Plan (NRRP), private investment has not fully rebounded to pre-pandemic levels. The IMF report stresses the potential for private sector investment to drive future growth, particularly in sectors focused on productivity enhancements and infrastructure.

Labor Market: Employment in Italy has recovered, with the unemployment rate dropping to 7.7% in 2023. However, skill shortages persist, with 45% of businesses reporting difficulty in hiring qualified workers. The demographic decline, exacerbated by low fertility rates and low female labor force participation, presents a challenge for Italy's future labor supply. Nevertheless, policies aimed at increasing labor force participation, particularly among women and older workers, are expected to improve employment prospects in the medium term.

Inflation and Price Stability: Heading Toward Target

Inflation in Italy has significantly decreased, with headline inflation falling to 0.9% in June 2024, driven by lower energy prices. Core inflation has also moderated, signaling price stability for the near term. The IMF projects inflation to stabilize at around 2% by 2025, aligning with the European Central Bank's target. However, risks remain, particularly if wage growth outpaces productivity or if energy prices rise unexpectedly.

Fiscal Policy: Navigating Debt Sustainability and Reforms

Italy's fiscal policy remains centered on reducing the public debt ratio, which, while improved from its peak of 155% of GDP in 2020, still poses a long-term risk. The IMF report underscores the need for Italy to adopt a more aggressive fiscal consolidation strategy to achieve a primary surplus of 3% of GDP by 2025-2026. Key fiscal reforms include narrowing tax exemptions, reducing inefficient spending, and gradually scaling back public guarantees.

Challenges in Fiscal Consolidation: Italy's fiscal space is constrained by growing expenditure pressures, particularly related to pensions and healthcare. While efforts to improve tax compliance and reduce the fiscal deficit are ongoing, the IMF cautions that more structural reforms are needed to ensure debt sustainability in the long term.

Investment Opportunities: Green Transition, Digitalization, and Infrastructure

Despite fiscal challenges, Italy offers significant investment opportunities in key sectors, particularly green energy, digital transformation, and infrastructure development.

Green Energy and Sustainability: Italy is positioning itself as a leader in Europe's green transition. With substantial investments in renewable energy, particularly solar and wind power, Italy is benefiting from the EU's Next Generation Funds to accelerate its energy transition. The IMF highlights growing opportunities in green technologies and energy efficiency projects, particularly for investors seeking sustainable returns.

Digital Transformation: Italy's digital economy is gaining momentum, with substantial investments in digital infrastructure and fintech. The IMF report points to growing opportunities in sectors like mobile payments, blockchain, and cybersecurity. Moreover, Italy's push for digital banking and public service digitization provides a favorable environment for innovation and tech-driven growth.

Infrastructure and Real Estate: Italy's infrastructure sector, especially in transportation, housing, and urban development, presents attractive opportunities for long-term investment. The IMF stresses the need for more affordable housing, with rising costs in major cities creating potential demand for new housing projects. Additionally, investments in public infrastructure, particularly those supported by the NRRP, offer steady returns for private capital.

Risks to Investment: Fiscal and Structural Challenges

While Italy offers a promising investment environment, several risks must be considered:

Political and Fiscal Uncertainty: Italy's fragmented political landscape and the high cost of debt continue to pose risks to economic stability. The IMF warns that delayed fiscal reforms and challenges in completing the NRRP could undermine investor confidence, particularly if fiscal deficits remain larger than pre-COVID levels.

Demographic Decline: Italy's shrinking working-age population and low fertility rates present a significant challenge to its labor market and long-term economic growth. Without significant reforms in education and workforce participation, the aging population will weigh on Italy's productivity and potential for sustained growth.

External Shocks: Italy's economy remains vulnerable to global economic risks, including geopolitical tensions, commodity price fluctuations, and trade disruptions. As a major exporter, Italy's dependence on the global economy makes it susceptible to external shocks.

Conclusion: A Resilient Economy with Promising Investment Potential

Italy's economy in 2024 is at a crossroads, presenting a mix of challenges and opportunities. While fiscal consolidation and structural reforms remain essential for long-term growth, Italy's focus on green energy, digitalization, and infrastructure provides a solid foundation for investment. For investors, Italy offers a balanced mix of opportunities, particularly in sectors aligned with the EU's green and digital ambitions.

As Italy continues to address its fiscal and structural challenges, it remains an attractive destination for investors seeking to align with Europe's green transition and technological transformation. The next few years will be crucial in determining whether Italy can maintain its economic resilience and capitalize on its investment potential.

This chapter integrates the key insights from the IMF staff consultation report on Italy's economic landscape, drawing attention to the challenges, opportunities, and risks that shape Italy's investment potential.

Chapter (9)

Canada: A Resilient Economy Amid Housing and Fiscal Challenges, Poised for Green Growth

Canada's economic outlook in 2024 is shaped by resilient growth, strategic fiscal measures, and a clear focus on the green transition. Despite challenges in housing affordability, productivity growth, and global uncertainties, the latest IMF consultation report highlights Canada's ability to navigate these complexities. With a strong labor market, ongoing fiscal reforms, and government-backed initiatives in critical sectors, the country remains a promising investment destination. Below, I delve into the details of Canada's current economic landscape, growth prospects, and areas of opportunity for investors.

Economic Performance: Resilient Growth Despite Structural Pressures

Canada has weathered global shocks, such as the COVID-19 pandemic and the global energy crisis, with relatively stable growth. However, challenges remain, particularly in housing affordability and productivity growth.

Gross Domestic Product (GDP) Growth: After a strong rebound in 2022, with GDP growing by 3.8%, Canada's growth moderated to 1.2% in 2023, largely due to a slowdown in private consumption and investment. Despite this, Canada's growth remained stronger than most G7 economies, supported by strong US demand and robust immigration inflows. Real GDP growth in 2024 is projected to pick up slightly to 1.3%, with consumption expected to grow by 2.8% year-on-year.

Inflation: Inflation, which peaked at 8% in mid-2022, has moderated to 2.9% in May 2024, falling within the Bank of Canada's target range of 1–3%. The decline in inflation has been driven by a contraction in domestic demand and tight monetary policy. However, shelter inflation remains high at 6.4%, reflecting continued increases in housing prices, rents, and mortgage rates.

Labor Market: Canada's labor market has remained resilient, with strong employment growth driven by immigration. However, the unemployment rate has risen slightly to 6.2% in 2024, above the estimated natural rate of 6%. The increase in immigration, which surged to 3.2% in 2023, has added to housing demand, exacerbating affordability issues. The IMF forecasts that labor market tightness will moderate as immigration flows soften.

Fiscal Strategy: Managing Debt and Addressing Housing Affordability

Canada's fiscal position remains relatively strong compared to other G7 countries, but the country faces significant challenges in managing debt and addressing long-term structural issues, especially in housing.

Fiscal Deficit and Debt: Canada's fiscal deficit in 2023 was modest, at 0.6% of potential GDP, with the general government gross debt at 107% of GDP. The IMF forecasts that public debt will decline to 95.2% of GDP by 2029. However, the government faces fiscal pressures, with spending on housing and climate policies expected to increase. Canada has committed to gradually reducing its debt-to-GDP ratio through fiscal consolidation.

Housing Crisis: The IMF report highlights that housing affordability has reached its worst levels in a generation. Despite rising housing starts in 2023, the supply of housing has failed to meet demand, fuelled by a surge in immigration. The government has set an ambitious target to build 3.9 million new homes by 2031, aiming to bridge the housing supply gap. However, the affordability crisis, particularly in rental markets, remains acute, with vacancy rates at historic lows and rents rising by 8% year-on-year in 2023.

Fiscal Policy Coordination: The IMF emphasizes the importance of coordinating fiscal policy with the Bank of Canada's monetary policy. Although Canada's fiscal space remains strong compared to other G7 nations, further fiscal restraint may be necessary in the short term to support inflation goals and rebuild fiscal buffers. The recent introduction of quantitative fiscal objectives is a positive step, with the government aiming to reduce the deficit to 1% of GDP by 2026/27.

Investment Horizons: Green Transition, Technology, and Housing Solutions

Canada's green transition and technological innovation are central to its economic strategy, offering substantial growth opportunities in various sectors.

Green Economy and Energy Transition: Canada's commitment to reducing greenhouse gas emissions by 40–45% by 2030 presents substantial investment opportunities in renewable energy and clean technology. Carbon pricing remains a central tool in the country's climate strategy, with the price of carbon set to rise to CAD 170 per tonne by 2030. The transition to a low-carbon economy offers significant growth potential in green industries, including renewable energy, electric vehicle manufacturing, and critical minerals.

Tech and Innovation: Canada's tech sector is poised for growth, particularly in areas like artificial intelligence, digital infrastructure, and clean technology. The government's focus on boosting productivity, including investment in R&D and green technology, aligns with its long-term economic goals. Investments in AI and digital infrastructure are expected to accelerate as Canada seeks to improve productivity and integrate advanced technologies into its economy.

Housing and Construction: The government's multi-faceted approach to solving the housing crisis presents investment opportunities in the construction and real estate development sectors. With a target of building nearly 4 million homes by 2031, construction and infrastructure investments will be critical to meeting the housing demand.

Investors in the real estate sector should monitor these developments, particularly in high-demand urban areas.

Risks and Opportunities: Global Risks and Domestic Challenges

While Canada's economic outlook remains positive, there are several risks that investors should monitor closely, particularly in housing, fiscal policy, and global trade.

Housing Affordability: The housing affordability crisis is likely to persist in the near term, despite government efforts to boost supply. While the 2024 federal budget allocated resources to support housing construction, the scale of the issue means that affordability will remain a significant challenge, especially in rental markets. Investors should focus on regions where demand is high, but also consider the long-term impact of housing policies and supply-side constraints.

Global Economic Risks: A global slowdown, particularly in major trading partners like the US, could dampen Canadian exports and economic growth. While Canada's economy remains resilient, the external environment remains a potential risk. Investors should also be cautious about commodity price fluctuations, given Canada's reliance on exports of oil, gas, and minerals.

Fiscal and Monetary Policy Risks: As Canada works toward fiscal consolidation, any misalignment between fiscal and monetary policies could slow down economic growth. The IMF highlights the need for continued fiscal discipline, particularly in managing public spending and raising revenues. Investors should monitor fiscal reforms and potential changes in tax policies, particularly those aimed at boosting green investments and housing affordability.

Strategic Takeaways for Investors:

Focus on Green and Digital Sectors: With a strong government commitment to sustainability and digital innovation, sectors related to renewable energy, electric vehicles, and AI present substantial growth opportunities.

Monitor Housing Policies: The ongoing housing affordability crisis offers opportunities in construction, real estate development, and infrastructure investments, particularly in urban areas with high demand.

Diversify Investments: Given the uncertainties around global economic risks and domestic fiscal challenges, a diversified investment strategy across sectors like tech, energy, and housing will help mitigate risks while capturing growth opportunities.

A Balanced Path to Sustainable Growth

Canada's economy stands at a crossroads, with significant challenges in housing affordability and fiscal management but also a clear commitment to sustainable growth through green technologies and digital innovation. With the government's focus on addressing structural issues and supporting key sectors, Canada remains an attractive destination for investors who can navigate the evolving landscape. By focusing on green energy, housing development, and technology, investors can position themselves to benefit from Canada's long-term growth potential, while managing the risks associated with global economic uncertainty and domestic policy challenges.

Chapter (10)

Brazil: A Green and Digital Economy on the Rise

Brazil's economic outlook in 2024 shines with resilience and innovation, thanks to strategic fiscal policies, a green-focused agenda, and digital transformation. The IMF's recent consultation report highlights Brazil's commitment to sustainable and inclusive growth, positioning the nation as an attractive destination for investors keen on green projects and fintech. Here, I delve deeper into Brazil's growth drivers, fiscal strategies, and notable investment opportunities.

Economic Vitality: Solid Growth and Inflation on a Steady Decline

Brazil has demonstrated strong growth despite global headwinds, with GDP expanding by 2.9% in 2023, driven by record agricultural and hydrocarbon outputs and resilient private consumption. This growth is expected to moderate to 2.1% in 2024, in part due to still-restrictive monetary policies, but projections for medium-term growth remain promising at 2.5% by 2027.

Inflation Control: The Central Bank's carefully managed monetary policies have reduced inflation, bringing it down to 3.9% year-over-year in May 2024, well within the target tolerance range. Inflation is expected to converge to the 3% target by 2026, signalling stability for investors and households alike.

Labor Market Strength: Unemployment in Brazil dropped to 7.5% by early 2024, its lowest rate since 2014. Employment gains across demographics have boosted private consumption, providing a stable foundation for economic growth and creating demand across various sectors.

Fiscal Fortitude: Balancing Public Spending with Debt Control

Brazil's fiscal strategy balances the need for public investment with debt management, targeting a federal primary deficit reduction from 2.4% of GDP in 2023 to 0.6% in 2024. Projections indicate Brazil will achieve a primary surplus of 1% of GDP by 2029, relying on increased tax revenue and moderated spending to reach fiscal goals.

Deficit Reduction Path: Revenue measures, including a VAT reform, are set to boost fiscal health. Additionally, a new fiscal rule allows controlled spending increases between 0.6% and 2.5% depending on revenue and primary balance targets, allowing Brazil the flexibility to prioritize spending in critical sectors while managing debt.

Fiscal Policy Innovations: Brazil's 2023 fiscal rule framework provides fiscal stability while encouraging investments in health, education, and infrastructure. Approved in 2023, the VAT reform streamlines federal and subnational VAT structures, boosting productivity and ensuring equitable taxation across sectors.

Bahaa G. Arnouk

Investment Horizons: Green Transition, Fintech Expansion, and Digital Innovation

Brazil's forward-looking green initiatives and groundbreaking digital finance systems present unique investment opportunities. The country's active approach to tackling deforestation, expanding its digital finance landscape, and promoting innovation in energy and technology demonstrates its commitment to sustainable and inclusive growth.

Deforestation Reduction and Ecological Transformation: Brazil's ambitious Ecological Transformation Plan is central to its green economy strategy, aiming to halt illegal deforestation by 2030. In 2023 alone, deforestation in the Amazon was reduced by a significant 50%, marking a milestone in Brazil's environmental policies. This reduction represents an estimated 0.5 gigaton reduction in carbon emissions, demonstrating Brazil's proactive stance on climate issues. The government has enhanced funding for IBAMA, the Brazilian Institute of Environment and Renewable Natural Resources, and established a carbon market, integrating cap-and-trade systems that set emission caps for companies releasing more than 25,000 tons of CO2 annually. Additionally, Brazil's new carbon trading framework now supports the voluntary carbon market, allowing credits from forest preservation projects to be traded globally, which attracts investment into carbon offset and reforestation projects.

Green Bond Issuances and Renewable Energy: The successful launch of Brazil's first green and social sovereign bond in November 2023 marked a major step toward green finance, creating a yield curve for green investments and expanding the market for sustainable projects. Plans are underway for another bond issuance, establishing Brazil as a key player in green finance. ECO Invest Brasil, a capital mobilization program, further supports these efforts by attracting foreign investments and providing FX hedging to promote green infrastructure and renewable energy development.

Digital Finance Innovation: PIX and Drex Leading the Way

Brazil's digital finance landscape has undergone a revolution, led by initiatives like Pix and Drex, positioning the nation at the forefront of financial inclusion and innovation. These digital tools have transformed how Brazilians interact with financial services, providing a secure and accessible platform for payments and, soon, digital currency.

Pix: Instantaneous Payment System: Launched by the Central Bank of Brazil in 2020, Pix is a free, real-time payment system that has seen exponential adoption, with over 25 million transactions processed daily. Pix's ability to facilitate instant transfers between bank accounts, regardless of the time or day, has made it immensely popular, especially among unbanked populations, small businesses, and individuals across socioeconomic segments. With Pix, Brazil has surpassed global averages in per capita digital transactions, significantly enhancing financial inclusion by reducing transaction costs, increasing transparency, and fostering competition. The Central Bank plans to expand Pix's capabilities, including automatic payments and cross-border functionality, although resource constraints have caused some delays.

Drex: Pioneering Central Bank Digital Currency (CBDC): Set to launch in 2025, Drex, Brazil's forthcoming digital currency, is designed to tokenize the economy by providing a public blockchain infrastructure, enabling secure, regulated financial services. Drex's infrastructure will allow for token-based financial services, helping individuals and businesses leverage digital assets as collateral for credit. Drex aims to support the credit system by allowing

78

tokenizable collateral (such as government bonds) to be used in innovative financing arrangements, increasing credit access for smaller borrowers and incentivizing new entrants in the financial services market. The Central Bank is addressing privacy and governance challenges to ensure the scalability and security of Drex. By enabling smart contract-based transactions and aiming for cross-border compatibility, Drex has the potential to become a model for digital currencies in emerging markets.

Managing Risks: A Pathway of Resilience Amid Global Challenges

While Brazil's growth prospects are strong, global uncertainties such as trade fluctuations, commodity price volatility, and domestic fiscal challenges remain on the horizon.

Global Economic Risks: Slowdowns in major trading partners like the U.S. or China could impact Brazilian exports, especially in agriculture and hydrocarbons. Commodity price volatility, particularly in oil and soybeans, could also affect Brazil's trade balance and fiscal health.

Fiscal Discipline and Inflation Alignment: Fiscal discipline will be crucial to Brazil's economic strategy, ensuring inflation remains within target ranges. The IMF underscores the importance of fiscal restraint to support monetary goals, with the Central Bank maintaining flexibility to manage inflation within target.

Strategic Insights for Investors:

Green Infrastructure and Renewable Projects: Brazil's Ecological Transformation Plan and aggressive deforestation reduction goals create significant opportunities in renewable energy, reforestation, and green bond markets.

Housing and Infrastructure Expansion: Post-disaster infrastructure needs, coupled with ongoing urbanization, present robust opportunities in construction and urban development.

Digital and Financial Services Growth: With Drex and Pix transforming Brazil's financial ecosystem, investments in fintech, digital services, and blockchain applications are positioned for growth.

Brazil's Green and Digital Future: A Balanced Approach to Sustainable Growth

Brazil's commitment to fiscal responsibility, environmental stewardship, and digital finance innovation underpins its economic strategy for 2024 and beyond. The nation's proactive approach to green finance, from deforestation efforts to carbon markets, combined with cutting-edge fintech initiatives like Pix and Drex, make Brazil an exciting destination for investors seeking to align with sustainable and digital growth. As Brazil continues its path toward economic inclusivity and resilience, investment opportunities in green energy, financial technology, and infrastructure are expected to yield long-term rewards for forward-thinking investors.

Bahaa G. Arnouk

Chapter (11)

South Korea's Economic Outlook: Navigating Growth, Debt, and Structural Challenges for a Sustainable Future

South Korea, Asia's fourth-largest economy, is recovering from the pandemic-induced slowdown while grappling with deeper structural challenges. The IMF's Article IV Consultation report for 2023 provides a comprehensive view of the country's economic trajectory, highlighting growth prospects, fiscal strategies, inflation concerns, and financial stability risks. Despite a modest recovery from recent disruptions, South Korea faces persistent challenges, including an aging population, rising public debt, and vulnerabilities in its financial sector. These factors require prudent policymaking and significant structural reforms to ensure long-term prosperity.

GDP Growth: Sluggish Recovery Amid External Challenges

South Korea's economy experienced a slowdown starting in mid-2022 as the global semiconductor cycle weakened, reducing demand for one of its key exports. The IMF's updated forecasts show a real GDP growth of 1.4% in 2023, followed by a more optimistic 2.2% in 2024. While global semiconductor demand is expected to recover, growth remains constrained by several external and internal factors.

The country's export sector, particularly in semiconductors, which constitutes a major portion of total exports, has faced severe pressure. The global semiconductor downcycle has had a cascading effect on trade, with South Korea's export volume growing only by 2.5% in 2023, lower than in previous years. Despite this, signs of stabilization are emerging, helped by strong domestic demand and improvements in global conditions.

In the medium term, South Korea's recovery will be bolstered by the anticipated rebound in semiconductor exports, the return of Chinese tourists, and stabilization in housing and domestic demand. However, the IMF report highlights significant risks tied to global factors such as higher global interest rates, slow global growth, and geopolitical tensions, particularly with China, South Korea's largest trading partner.

Public Debt and Fiscal Outlook: Tightening the Belt for Long-Term Sustainability

South Korea's fiscal policy is currently focused on normalizing after pandemic-era stimulus measures, with the IMF projecting a decline in the fiscal deficit from 3.0% of GDP in 2022 to 1.8% in 2023. However, the nation's public debt, which stood at 49.3% of GDP in 2023, is expected to rise further, placing pressure on fiscal sustainability over the longer term. As the country faces an aging population and rising pension liabilities, managing public finances is a delicate balancing act.

The government is pursuing fiscal consolidation by focusing on reducing the fiscal deficit, but revenue shortfalls in 2023—largely due to weak corporate tax and property tax revenues—have made this challenging. The IMF recommends the continued use of government reserves to cover these gaps, but emphasizes the need for substantial fiscal reforms to address the underlying issue of an aging population, which is expected to increase pension spending significantly over the coming decades.

To maintain fiscal health, the IMF suggests the adoption of a rules-based fiscal framework, which would include a debt ceiling of 60% of GDP and a balanced fiscal budget. However, the report notes that these fiscal rules should allow for flexibility to counteract economic downturns, ensuring that South Korea has room to implement counter-cyclical policies when necessary.

Inflation: Moderation Expected but Core Pressures Persist

Inflation in South Korea has moderated from its 2022 peak, but core inflation—excluding food and energy—remains elevated. In 2023, the inflation rate is projected to reach 3.6% on average, easing further to 2.4% in 2024, approaching the Bank of Korea's target of 2. A major contributor to inflation in 2022 was the sharp rise in global energy prices, which impacted domestic inflation. By 2023, energy and food prices have started to decline, bringing down headline inflation, but core inflation has remained persistent, driven by strong domestic demand, rising wages, and supply-side constraints.

The Bank of Korea (BoK) has kept the policy rate at 3.5%, above neutral levels, to curb inflationary pressures. The BoK's monetary stance remains tight, and the IMF advises that any future rate cuts should only occur in response to clear signs of inflation slowing or a significant economic downturn.

Household Debt and Financial Vulnerability: A Growing Risk

One of the most pressing concerns for South Korea is the rising household debt, which is among the highest in the OECD. Household debt has increased to approximately 101.7% of GDP in mid-2023. This situation is exacerbated by high levels of floating-rate debt, which makes households more vulnerable to interest rate hikes. The IMF notes that while South Korea's financial sector remains relatively resilient, financial vulnerabilities have emerged, particularly within households and certain sectors like real estate and construction.

Rising household debt, in combination with a weakening housing market, has contributed to a fragile financial situation for many South Korean families. Housing prices, which surged during the pandemic, have started to decline, leading to a situation where Jeonse deposit risks (a unique form of rental deposit system in Korea) are increasing. The IMF warns that these risks could result in greater financial distress for households, especially if economic conditions worsen or interest rates stay elevated.

The government has responded by tightening regulations on mortgage lending and introducing temporary measures to ease debt repayment stress, such as mortgage support programs and targeted housing assistance. However, the IMF cautions that these measures should remain temporary and targeted, as prolonged intervention risks exacerbating moral hazard and further inflating household debt.

Investment Landscape: Structural Reforms for Innovation and Productivity

South Korea remains a strong investment hub, particularly in technology and manufacturing sectors. However, to ensure sustained long-term growth, the country needs to tackle several structural challenges, including improving productivity growth, fostering innovation in services, and addressing demographic changes.

A key concern is the relatively slow pace of innovation in the service sector, where small businesses dominate. The government is working on policies to level the playing field between services and manufacturing, lower barriers to entry, and reduce the complexity of the regulatory environment for startups. Additionally, the labor market requires reform to improve flexibility and reduce rigidities, particularly in terms of wage systems and working hours. The government's ongoing efforts to address gender gaps in labor market participation are also critical for enhancing productivity.

The IMF also highlights the need for South Korea to increase its investment in green technologies and strengthen its commitment to climate change mitigation, as the country has ambitious goals for carbon neutrality by 2050. This includes reforming the Emissions Trading Scheme (ETS) and raising carbon pricing to incentivize greener practices across industries.

Risks to Growth and Stability: External and Domestic Pressures

Despite a relatively strong economic foundation, South Korea faces significant risks that could derail its recovery. These risks are both external—such as global economic downturns, trade disruptions, and geopolitical tensions—and domestic, including financial market instability, rising household debt, and the demographic pressures from an aging population.

The IMF identifies several downside risks to the economic outlook, including tighter global monetary policy, rising commodity prices, and vulnerabilities in the financial sector. Additionally, the ongoing geoeconomic fragmentation could affect South Korea's trade relations, particularly with China and the US.

Conclusion: A Path of Caution and Reform

South Korea's economic outlook is cautiously optimistic, but the road to sustainable long-term growth will require careful management of both fiscal policies and structural reforms.

With a significant public debt burden, high household debt, and an aging population, the country must focus on maintaining fiscal prudence while reforming its labor market, pension system, and investment climate to foster innovation.

The IMF's recommendations point to the need for continued fiscal consolidation, addressing the risks of rising debt, and supporting financial stability. It also calls for more ambitious reforms in the labor market and pension systems to ensure future prosperity. While external risks remain, South Korea has the tools to mitigate these challenges—if it acts decisively and maintains a steady course of policy reform and innovation.

By leveraging its strengths in technology, innovation, and exports, and addressing key vulnerabilities in the financial system, South Korea can continue to grow as a leading global economy, but only if it navigates these hurdles with careful policy execution and foresight.

Chapter (12)

Mexico: A Roadmap for Economic Resilience and Investment Amid Challenges

Mexico's economic outlook in 2024 is a testament to its resilience in the face of global uncertainties, with strategic fiscal policies, a strong fiscal framework, and a renewed focus on sustainability and innovation. As outlined in the IMF's 2024 consultation report, the country is experiencing moderated growth, addressing key fiscal pressures, and planning for long-term sustainability. Despite challenges such as public debt concerns and corruption, Mexico's forward-looking policies offer promising investment opportunities. In this chapter, we will explore Mexico's economic landscape in detail, focusing on key measures, fiscal strategies, and investment prospects.

Economic Outlook: Navigating Growth Amid Constraints

Mexico's economic performance in 2023 showed resilience, with a 3.2% GDP growth driven by robust manufacturing and construction sectors, as well as strong exports to the United States. However, as we move into 2024, growth is projected to slow down significantly, with the IMF forecasting a more modest 1.5% expansion. The slowdown is attributed to ongoing capacity constraints and restrictive monetary policies, which are expected to take a toll on private consumption and investment.

Real GDP Growth: While 2023 demonstrated impressive performance, 2024 will see a significant deceleration in growth. This moderation is driven by slower economic momentum in key sectors and external factors, including a weaker U.S. economy and a tightening of fiscal policies. The IMF expects the growth to further moderate in 2025, with a long-term potential growth rate around 2%.

Inflation Management: Inflation remains one of Mexico's most pressing issues. By September 2024, inflation stood at 4.6% year-over-year, above the central bank's target of 3%. While core inflation (which excludes volatile food and energy prices) is falling, services inflation remains sticky, largely due to rising wages and operational costs in certain sectors. However, Banxico (the Central Bank of Mexico) has managed to steer inflation expectations back on track through a series of policy rate hikes, and inflation is expected to converge to the 3% target by the end of 2025. The IMF has called for a gradual, data-driven approach to further monetary easing.

Fiscal Policy and Public Debt: Striking a Balance Between Stimulus and Consolidation

Mexico's fiscal policy in 2024 is notably procyclical, with an expected deficit of 5.9% of GDP, up from 4.3% in 2023.

The IMF has highlighted the need for a frontloaded fiscal consolidation in 2025 to restore fiscal sustainability. However, this will require substantial fiscal reforms and careful expenditure management to avoid worsening the country's debt profile.

Public Debt Dynamics: Public debt in Mexico is on an upward trajectory, projected to reach 58% of GDP by the end of 2024. While the debt level remains moderate compared to other emerging markets, it poses a risk if not managed properly. The IMF underscores the importance of implementing fiscal reforms to stabilize debt over the medium term. Without these reforms, Mexico risks a growing fiscal deficit that could lead to higher borrowing costs and reduced fiscal space to respond to future shocks.

Fiscal Deficit and Adjustment: To curb public debt, the Mexican government has set ambitious fiscal consolidation targets. The deficit is expected to reduce to below 3% of GDP by 2026. The IMF recommends tax reforms to increase non-oil revenues and reduce reliance on volatile oil revenues. Reforms are necessary to broaden the tax base, improve tax collection, and streamline inefficient tax expenditures, which currently hinder the government's ability to finance critical investments in infrastructure, health, and education.

Pemex and State-Owned Enterprises: A significant portion of Mexico's fiscal pressure stems from state-owned enterprises, notably Pemex. While the oil company remains a cornerstone of Mexico's energy policy, its financial burden on the government is substantial. The IMF advises that support for Pemex should be conditional on meaningful corporate governance reforms and strategic adjustments. Mexico's reliance on Pemex is a critical risk factor, especially in an era of fluctuating global oil prices.

Challenges: Corruption, Fiscal Discipline, and Governance Issues

Despite strong macroeconomic fundamentals and a favourable external position, Mexico faces significant challenges that could undermine its economic growth and investment potential. Corruption, governance issues, and a need for deeper fiscal reforms are some of the most pressing concerns.

Corruption and Rule of Law: Corruption remains a pervasive issue in Mexico, and it continues to have a direct impact on the business climate and public finances. According to the IMF, crime, corruption, and weak rule of law are significant barriers to investment. These issues exacerbate operating costs for businesses and deter foreign investors. The IMF has urged the Mexican government to address these structural weaknesses through comprehensive legal reforms, including strengthening the judiciary and improving the transparency of public procurement processes.

Judicial and Legal Reforms: Mexico's recent constitutional amendments to the judiciary are intended to increase accountability but have raised concerns about judicial independence. These changes are still in the early stages, and the IMF has called for safeguards to ensure the independence and professionalism of the judiciary. Without these safeguards, the legal environment could become more unpredictable, further deterring investment.

Fiscal Reforms and Tax Evasion: The need for a robust fiscal framework remains urgent. Mexico's tax revenue is relatively low, especially compared to OECD peers, constraining the government's ability to invest in infrastructure, healthcare, and education. Efforts to reform tax administration are underway, but challenges remain. In particular, the IMF highlights the need to combat tax evasion, improve the efficiency of public expenditure, and implement a more comprehensive medium-term budget framework. The government's capacity to raise revenue through effective taxation is crucial to its fiscal consolidation plan.

Investment Horizons: Sectors Primed for Growth

Despite these challenges, Mexico presents a wealth of opportunities for investors, particularly in sectors such as green energy, manufacturing, and fintech. Mexico's integration into global supply chains, its strategic location next to the U.S., and its growing tech sector provide fertile ground for investment.

Green Energy: Mexico's commitment to environmental sustainability presents significant opportunities in renewable energy. The country is increasingly focusing on solar, wind, and geothermal energy projects to diversify its energy mix and reduce dependency on fossil fuels. The government is also working to attract foreign investments in clean energy infrastructure, particularly in the context of global climate commitments and the growing demand for sustainable energy.

Fintech and Digital Transformation: Mexico's fintech sector has been gaining momentum, with digital banking, mobile payments, and blockchain technology becoming integral to the country's financial ecosystem. With low financial inclusion rates, particularly in rural areas, there is vast potential for growth in digital financial services. The government is also making strides in improving digital infrastructure, which will further open up the market for fintech companies and digital investors.

Manufacturing and Trade: The relocation of global supply chains, coupled with Mexico's favorable trade agreements like the USMCA (United States-Mexico-Canada Agreement), positions the country as a key player in global manufacturing. With a strategic location next to the U.S. market, Mexico has become an increasingly attractive destination for foreign direct investment (FDI), particularly in the automotive, electronics, and medical device industries.

Infrastructure Development: There is a significant demand for infrastructure investment in Mexico, driven by urbanization, the need for transportation improvements, and ongoing public-private partnerships. The government's focus on improving infrastructure in the southern regions and connecting rural areas to the rest of the economy presents opportunities in logistics, construction, and urban development.

Risks and Mitigation: Preparing for Uncertainties

While Mexico's growth prospects are strong, there are several risks that could affect its trajectory:

Global Economic Uncertainty: Fluctuations in U.S. demand, changes in global financial market conditions, and rising commodity prices could negatively impact Mexico's trade and investment flows. The IMF has identified these as significant external risks, which could lead to a slowdown in economic activity.

Monetary and Fiscal Policy Coordination: The IMF stresses the importance of continued fiscal discipline in maintaining investor confidence. Without a credible fiscal adjustment plan, Mexico could face higher borrowing costs, potentially limiting fiscal flexibility.

Conclusion: Mexico's Path to Economic Sustainability and Investment Growth

Mexico stands at a crossroads, balancing the challenges of fiscal consolidation, inflation control, and governance reforms with promising growth opportunities in green energy, fintech, and infrastructure. While the road ahead may be fraught with challenges—particularly around public debt and corruption—the country's strong macroeconomic policy frameworks, strategic location, and investment-friendly sectors make it an attractive destination for long-term investment.

The IMF's 2024 consultation highlights the importance of a coordinated effort between fiscal policy reforms, anti-corruption measures, and continued investment in key sectors to secure sustainable growth for Mexico. As the country navigates these complex dynamics, it remains a prime destination for investors looking for growth in a rapidly changing global economy.

Chapter (13)

Australia: Economic Resilience Amidst Challenges, with Focus on Productivity, Inflation Control, and Green Transformation

Australia's post-pandemic recovery has been notably resilient, outpacing many of its peers. However, as the country enters 2024, it faces a delicate balancing act— managing high inflation, slowing growth, and the ongoing challenge of productivity stagnation. The IMF's 2023 staff report outlines an economic trajectory marked by fiscal discipline, monetary tightening, and strategic investments in green transformation and digital infrastructure. For investors, Australia's evolving landscape presents a mix of near-term hurdles and long-term opportunities.

Economic Growth Slows, But Resilience Remains

Australia's economy has proven resilient in the post-pandemic period, though it faces headwinds in 2024 and beyond. The IMF's projections highlight a gradual deceleration in growth due to the tightening of monetary conditions and broader global uncertainties:

Growth Projections: Real GDP growth is expected to slow to **1.8% in 2023** and further decelerate to **1.4% in 2024**, with the primary drag coming from weaker household consumption. The slowdown is exacerbated by higher interest rates, which have hurt disposable incomes and increased the cost of living

Private Consumption: As mortgage rates rise and real wages remain stagnant, household consumption has been subdued. In particular, private consumption is expected to grow by just 0.8% in 2024, a sharp contrast to the robust 6.5% growth seen in 2022.

Investment Resilience: On a positive note, **business investment** remains strong, supported by government incentives and fiscal measures. Private investment is projected to grow by **6.7% in 2023**, while **public investment**—particularly in infrastructure—remains a key pillar of growth.

Inflation d Fiscal Tightening: A Delicate Balance

Australia faces persistently high inflation, though recent efforts to tighten fiscal and monetary policies are expected to curb price growth over the medium term:

Inflation Outlook: After peaking at **7.8% in Q4 2022**, inflation has moderated to **5.4% in Q3 2023**. However, it remains well above the **2-3% target** of the Reserve Bank of Australia (RBA). Inflationary pressures are driven by the services sector, including food and housing costs, alongside persistent demand in the labor market.

Monetary Policy: RBA has raised interest rates significantly since May 2022, bringing the **cash rate to 4.35%** by the end of 2023. The IMF suggests that further tightening may be needed to ensure inflation returns to target by **2025**, though this will depend on the speed of monetary policy transmission. .

Fiscal policy: government has implemented targeted fiscal consolidation, which has helped bring the budget deficit down. However, with inflation still elevated, **fiscal policy must continue tightening** to complement the RBA's efforts in managing demand and controlling price pressures. The cyclically adjusted primary is projected to turn positive by **2030**, but the IMF warns that further fiscal discipline is crucial to prevent inflation from becoming entrenched.

Green Transformation: Australia's Sustainable Future

Australia's green transformation efforts are a central part of its long-term economic strategy. As part of its goal to meet net-zero emissions by 2050, the country is investing heavily in renewable energy and sustainable infrastructure:

Renewable Energy: Australia is ramping up investments in **solar, wind, and hydrogen energy**. The government's **Clean Energy Target** and various subsidies are designed to attract private investments into the green energy sector. With the global shift toward cleaner energy, these sectors represent a compelling opportunity for investors.

Sustainable Infrastructure: Beyond Australia is focusing on sustainable urban development and eco-friendly technologies in transportation and housing. Investments in green buildings, electric vehicle (EV) infrastructure, and energy-efficient public transit are expected to grow significantly in the coming years.

Labor Market and Productivity: The Key Term Growth

While Australia's labor market remains strong, **productivity growth** has stagnated, posing risks to the country's long-term economic trajectory:

Labor Market: The **unemployment rate** has remained historically low, hovering at **3.7%** as of September 2023. However, **tight labor market conditions** are contributing to wage inflation, which in turn drives up costs for businesses and consumers alike. The IMF expects **unemployment** to rise up to **4.2% in 2024**, as economic activity slows .

Productivity Growth: The slow productivity Australia's most significant long-term challenge. The IMF stresses the need for structural reforms to address this stagnation, including investing in **digital infrastructure, research and development (R&D)**, and improving **education** to enhance skills. Additionally, labor market reforms to boost participation, especially among women and older workers, will be crucial.

Migration: Strong migration flows, particular led labor, are expected to alleviate some of the labor market tightness. Net migration increased by 2.2% in 2023, and continued high levels of immigration are expected to ease pressure on labor markets while also contributing to demand in sectors like housing.

Real Estate and Housing Market: A Tight Market with Rising prices

The Australian housing market has experienced significant fluctuations in recent years, with prices rising again after a sharp drop in 2022:

Housing Market Outlook: After a decline of around **8% between Q1 2022 and Q1 2023**, housing prices have begun to recover, driven by **strong demand, limited supply**, and **higher immigration**. However, this recovery is fragile and concentrated in certain segments, such as high-end properties in cities like Sydney.

Affordability Concerns: Housing affordability remains a key concern particularly in the rental market. The **rental inflation** rate has surged, exacerbating pressures on low-income households. The IMF suggests additional measures to increase housing supply and improve affordability, alongside potential changes to **tax policies** to address demand and supply imbalances.

Strategic Investment Takeaways: Green Transformation and Productivity

Investors looking to capitalize on Australia's economic evolution should focus on the sectors most aligned with the country's long-term goals:

Green Transformation: With substantial investments in renewable energy, infrastructure resilience, and sustainability, the green transformation sector offers attractive growth opportunities. The Australian government's commitment to achieving net-zero emissions by 2050 will continue to drive investment in this space.

Digital and Technological Innovation: As Australia seeks to boost its pr, sectors related to AI, automation, and digital infrastructure are poised for growth. Investment in R&D and technology-driven industries will be key to overcoming Australia's productivity challenges.

Infrastructure and Urban Development: Infrastructure projects, especially those sustainability and resilience, will remain a key driver of growth. Investors in sectors such as green construction and EV infrastructure can benefit from the government's continued focus on these areas.

Conclusion: A Strategic Foundation for Long-Term Investment

Australia's economic trajectory a unique mix of near-term challenges and long-term opportunities. With fiscal consolidation efforts, ongoing monetary tightening, and significant investments in green and digital transformations, the country is positioning itself for sustainable growth. Investors should consider targeting green technologies, digital innovation, and sustainable infrastructure projects, while remaining mindful of inflationary pressures and potential fiscal challenges. With the right strategic approach,

Australia's evolving economic landscape offers a robust foundation for long-term investment.

This chapter emphasized Australia's immediate economic outlook, along with the projections and fiscal policies in place to guide the economy in the coming years. By focusing on the IMF's detailed growth forecasts and sectoral opportunities.

Chapter (14)

Spain: A Recovering Economy with Growing Investment Potential Amid Challenges

Spain's economy in 2024 reflects a remarkable balance between resilience and challenges, with a clear focus on fiscal consolidation, a green energy transition, and digital transformation. Despite facing political fragmentation and structural vulnerabilities, Spain offers a robust investment landscape that promises long-term growth for those who align with its strategic objectives. The IMF's recent consultation report sheds light on Spain's progress, as well as the investment opportunities and risks that come with its trajectory over the next few years.

Economic Outlook: Resilience Amid Uncertainty

Spain's economic outlook for 2024 remains favorable, with real GDP growth projected to reach 2.4%. After a solid 2.5% expansion in 2023, driven by resilient domestic consumption, services exports, and public spending, Spain's economy is expected to moderate slightly in 2024 but remain strong compared to the Eurozone average. However, key risks persist, including political fragmentation, global

102

geopolitical tensions, and the potential under-execution of European recovery funds.

Private Consumption and Investment: Household consumption, which has been bolstered by strong wage growth and a reduction in unemployment, is expected to continue supporting the economy. However, private investment is still lagging below pre-pandemic levels. The IMF highlights that despite easing financial conditions, investment remains below expectations, especially in the corporate sector. This creates a window of opportunity for private sector investment to accelerate the pace of growth, particularly in productivity-enhancing sectors.

Labor Market: Spain's labor market has shown resilience, with employment growth continuing, albeit at a slower pace. The unemployment rate has declined to just below 12%, but structural unemployment remains the highest in the Eurozone. The reduction of temporary contracts, supported by labor market reforms in 2021, has provided stability to the workforce, but challenges remain in addressing the skills mismatch and improving labor force participation, particularly among older workers.

Inflation and Price Stability: Heading Toward ECB Targets

Inflation in Spain has significantly moderated from the peaks of 2022, with headline inflation dropping to 3.4% in 2023, down from 8.3% in 2022. Core inflation, which excludes energy and food prices, has also been on a steady decline. The IMF projects both headline and core inflation to converge towards the European Central Bank's (ECB) 2% target by mid-2025.

This decline in inflation is critical for creating a stable environment for investment. However, the IMF warns that inflation could face upside risks due to potential wage increases driven by the tight labor market and external factors such as global energy prices. While inflation pressures may recede in the medium term, investors must be aware of potential volatility in energy prices and labor costs that could affect the broader economic climate.

Fiscal Policy: Balancing Consolidation with Growth Support

Spain's fiscal policy remains centered on reducing the budget deficit and public debt, which stood at a high 107.7% of GDP in 2023. The IMF highlights that Spain's fiscal consolidation is progressing, but the path ahead remains challenging. The fiscal deficit fell from 4.7% of GDP in 2022 to 3.6% in 2023, and the government aims to reduce it further to 3% in 2024.

Challenges in Fiscal Consolidation: The IMF stresses the need for Spain to adopt a medium-term fiscal consolidation plan to achieve debt sustainability. The country faces growing public expenditure pressures, particularly in pensions and health care, due to an aging population. While revenue measures, such as increased taxes on income and social security contributions, have supported fiscal improvements, the IMF warns that without substantial reform in spending, particularly in the pension system, Spain may face fiscal strain in the long term.

Political Risks: Spain's fiscal trajectory is heavily influenced by its political landscape. The IMF points out that the fragmented political environment, marked by difficulties in passing legislation, could undermine the effectiveness of fiscal policies. The inability to pass a budget law for 2024 exemplifies the challenges ahead. Moreover, the lack of a clear medium-term fiscal plan has raised concerns about the sustainability of fiscal consolidation efforts.

Investment Opportunities: Green Transition, Digitalization, and Infrastructure

Despite the fiscal and political challenges, Spain presents significant investment opportunities, particularly in green energy, digital transformation, and infrastructure.

Green Transition and Renewable Energy: Spain's commitment to the green transition is a key driver of investment opportunities. The country has made substantial strides in renewable energy, especially in solar and wind power, and is positioning itself as a leader in clean energy within Europe. The IMF report highlights that Spain is benefitting from Next Generation EU (NGEU) funds, which are being used to accelerate green investments, including energy efficiency, clean technology, and sustainable infrastructure.

Green Bonds and Sustainable Finance: Spain's green bond market has become increasingly attractive to investors. The country's use of green bonds to finance renewable energy projects and infrastructure initiatives provides a growing opportunity for investors seeking sustainable returns. Furthermore, Spain's commitment to environmental sustainability, backed by the EU's green policies, offers a favorable environment for investment in green technologies and projects aimed at reducing carbon emissions.

Digital Economy and Innovation: Spain is also accelerating its digital transformation, with substantial investments in technology, fintech, and digital infrastructure. The IMF notes that Spain's digitalization efforts are being driven by both private and public sector investments, particularly in the financial sector. Initiatives like the digitization of public services and the push for digital banking provide robust opportunities in fintech and cybersecurity.

Fintech Growth: Spain's digital finance landscape, supported by NGEU funds, presents strong growth opportunities in the fintech sector. With Spain's growing emphasis on financial inclusion and digital payment systems, including the development of advanced digital payment infrastructure, investors can capitalize on opportunities in mobile payments, blockchain, and cybersecurity solutions.

Infrastructure Investment: Spain's infrastructure sector, particularly in transportation, urban development, and housing, also presents a significant opportunity for investment. The IMF highlights the need to increase the housing supply in Spain, as rising housing costs, especially in major cities, continue to strain affordability. Expanding affordable housing and investing in public infrastructure development present attractive avenues for private capital, particularly for long-term investors.

Risks to Investment: Political and Structural Challenges

While Spain offers compelling investment opportunities, several risks must be considered by potential investors.

Political Fragmentation: As mentioned, Spain's fragmented political landscape poses risks to the stability and implementation of economic policies. The inability to pass a budget and secure political consensus on key reforms, such as pension and tax policy changes, could create uncertainty for businesses and investors.

Fiscal and Debt Pressures: Spain's high public debt and rising social spending, especially in pensions, create long-term fiscal challenges. Without structural reforms to control spending and increase revenue, Spain's fiscal health could deteriorate, leading to higher borrowing costs and reduced investor confidence.

Global Risks: Spain's economy is also vulnerable to global economic conditions, including commodity price fluctuations, geopolitical tensions, and global trade disruptions. As a major exporter of goods and services, Spain is highly dependent on the global economic climate, making it susceptible to external shocks.

Conclusion: A Mixed but Promising Investment Landscape

Spain's economy in 2024 is at a crossroads, offering a mix of resilience and challenges. The country's strong fiscal consolidation efforts, vibrant green transition, and digital transformation provide a solid foundation for long-term growth. However, Spain's political fragmentation and the need for deeper structural reforms, particularly in the labor market and pension system, pose risks to its trajectory.

For investors, Spain presents a compelling case, particularly in the sectors of renewable energy, digital finance, and infrastructure. While political and fiscal risks persist, Spain's commitment to sustainable growth and technological innovation makes it an attractive destination for investors looking to align with the EU's green and digital ambitions.

As Spain continues to address its structural challenges, the next few years will be crucial in determining whether it can capitalize on its strengths and maintain its upward trajectory. For now, Spain offers a balanced mix of opportunities and risks for forward-thinking investors.

Chapter (15)

Indonesia's Economic Outlook: Growth, Debt, and the Road to High-Income Status

Indonesia, the largest economy in Southeast Asia, has been navigating a complex set of global challenges and domestic reforms. As the country aims to transition to a high-income status by 2045, it faces a delicate balancing act between pursuing growth and maintaining fiscal and financial stability. The IMF's latest Article IV consultation highlights Indonesia's robust economic performance, resilience against external shocks, and the pivotal role of structural reforms in shaping the future.

GDP Growth: Resilient but Constrained by External Headwinds

Indonesia's economy has shown strong resilience despite global headwinds. The country's real GDP growth was 5.0% in 2023, slightly below the 5.3% growth in 2022. In 2024, growth is expected to remain stable at 5.0%, with a slight increase to 5.1% in 2025. This growth trajectory is driven primarily by strong domestic demand, notably private consumption, which is forecast to increase by 4.9% in 2024 and 5.1% in 2025. Investment in gross fixed capital formation is projected to grow at 4.4% in 2024, accelerating slightly to 5.0% in 2025.

However, Indonesia's export sector faces challenges. Net exports, which contributed 0.8 percentage points to GDP growth in 2022, are expected to slow in the medium term. In 2024, real exports are projected to grow at a slower pace due to the softening of commodity prices and weaker global demand, particularly from its key trading partners. The current account deficit, which moved from a surplus of 1.0% of GDP in 2022 to a small deficit of 0.1% of GDP in 2023, is expected to widen to -0.9% of GDP in 2024, primarily due to this slower export growth.

Despite these challenges, the growth outlook remains positive, supported by domestic consumption and investment. The output gap, which stood at -0.3% of GDP in 2023, is expected to close by 2026, signaling that the economy will operate closer to its potential in the medium term.

Public Debt: Managing Fiscal Prudence Amid Expansionary Policies

Indonesia's fiscal discipline remains a key strength. The general government debt-to-GDP ratio stood at 39.6% in 2023, slightly down from 40.1% in 2022, well within the legal ceiling of 60%. This low debt ratio is a result of prudent fiscal management and a gradual reduction in the debt-to-GDP ratio over the past few years. The general government fiscal deficit decreased to 1.6% of GDP in 2023, down from 2.2%

in 2022, showing a continued commitment to fiscal consolidation post-pandemic.

In 2024, the fiscal deficit is projected to widen slightly to 2.3% of GDP, but it remains well within the fiscal rule's 3% limit. This expansionary fiscal stance, which will increase government spending on capital investments and social assistance, will add 0.8 percentage points of GDP to the fiscal impulse. The fiscal deficit is expected to remain moderately expansionary in 2025, with the deficit projected at 2.6% of GDP, gradually consolidating thereafter as the government looks to stabilize debt levels.

The primary balance turned positive in 2023, recording a surplus of 0.5% of GDP for the first time in nearly a decade, following a long period of fiscal consolidation. However, as government spending increases in 2024, the primary balance is expected to turn negative again at -0.3% of GDP, reflecting the need for additional fiscal support to sustain growth amidst global uncertainties.

Importantly, the government's debt service-to-revenue ratio remains high at approximately 13%, which is significantly above the median for emerging markets. This means that while Indonesia's overall debt levels are manageable, its ability to generate revenues to service this debt is constrained. Efforts to enhance revenue mobilization through tax reforms will be crucial in alleviating this pressure in the future.

Investment Landscape: The Need for Structural Reforms

Indonesia's investment landscape presents both opportunities and challenges. The country's rich natural resources, growing middle class, and significant infrastructure development plans, including the construction of the new capital city, Nusantara, provide ample opportunities for foreign direct investment (FDI). In 2023, FDI inflows amounted to $21.8 billion, representing around 1.5% of GDP. FDI inflows are projected to rise further in the medium term as infrastructure projects and economic reforms continue to unfold.

However, Indonesia faces several challenges in maintaining a favorable investment climate. One of the key concerns is the relatively low tax-to-GDP ratio, which stood at 13% in 2023, far below the regional average. The government has set ambitious targets for revenue mobilization, aiming to increase the tax-to-GDP ratio by 10 percentage points by 2045. This will require significant structural reforms in tax policy and administration. Proposals for a new National Revenue Agency (NRA), alongside digitalization and improvements in compliance enforcement, are expected to improve tax collection, but these measures need to be carefully implemented to avoid undermining business confidence.

Further structural reforms are required to address inefficiencies in the labor market, improve governance, and reduce corruption. These reforms are essential not only to attract investment but also to ensure that growth benefits are shared more inclusively across society. Indonesia's industrial policies should target market failures without distorting trade and investment flows. Transitioning away from non-tariff barriers and simplifying regulatory processes will be crucial for enhancing the country's global competitiveness.

Risks to Growth and Fiscal Stability

Despite the positive outlook, Indonesia faces significant risks. External risks include commodity price volatility, particularly in oil and gas, as well as the potential for a global slowdown or recession in key trading partners such as China and the US. In 2024, the trade balance, which saw a surplus of $46.5 billion in 2023, is expected to narrow as export growth slows and import growth picks up in line with domestic demand. The current account deficit is projected to widen, reaching -0.9% of GDP in 2024, before stabilizing in the medium term.

On the domestic front, the risks stem from the potential weakening of Indonesia's long-standing fiscal frameworks, particularly if the government fails to implement necessary tax reforms or if spending continues to outpace revenue generation. The IMF cautions that failure to adhere to fiscal discipline could undermine policy credibility and increase debt service pressures.

Indonesia also faces risks related to global geopolitical tensions, which could disrupt supply chains, increase inflation, or lead to a rapid depreciation of the rupiah. While the central bank, Bank Indonesia (BI), has successfully managed inflation within its target range of 3% ± 1% in recent years, external shocks—particularly from rising US

interest rates—could test the effectiveness of the country's
monetary policy.

The Road Ahead: Achieving High-Income Status

Indonesia's ambitious goal of reaching high-income status by
2045 requires a transformative approach. The government's
"Golden Vision" outlines key reforms necessary to shift
from a commodity-dependent economy to one based on
high-value-added manufacturing and a skilled workforce. To
achieve this vision, Indonesia will need to significantly boost
infrastructure investment, improve the quality of education,
and reduce barriers to trade and investment.

Achieving high-income status will also require addressing the
country's social and environmental challenges. The IMF's
report highlights the importance of strengthening social
protection programs and ensuring that growth is inclusive.
Furthermore, Indonesia's climate goals, including a target of
net-zero emissions by 2060, will require substantial
investment in renewable energy and carbon-reduction
initiatives.

Achieving these goals will not be easy. Structural reforms will
be necessary to enhance governance, improve public
services, and tackle the barriers that currently limit
productivity growth. This will also require strengthening the
financial sector, enhancing fiscal management, and boosting
international trade relations.

In conclusion, while Indonesia is on a promising growth
path, it must remain vigilant to external and domestic risks.
With careful management of its fiscal policies, investment in

structural reforms, and resilience in the face of global uncertainties, Indonesia has the potential to achieve its vision of becoming a high-income country by 2045. But, as with all ambitious plans, the road ahead will require significant effort and careful policy execution to overcome the risks that lie ahead.

Chapter (16)

Turkey's Economic Outlook for 2025 and Beyond: Key Challenges and Growth Prospects

Turkey's economy has made significant strides toward recovery after a tumultuous period of high inflation, fiscal imbalances, and currency depreciation in 2023. A series of decisive policy shifts, including monetary tightening and fiscal reforms, have laid the foundation for Turkey's economic stabilization. However, challenges remain, and a full recovery will depend on Turkey's ability to manage inflation, fiscal deficits, and public debt while maintaining investor confidence.

This analysis delves into Turkey's GDP growth, public debt dynamics, fiscal deficit, inflation trajectory, and the key risks that investors must consider moving forward, with particular attention to the policies outlined in the IMF's 2024 Article IV Consultation report.

GDP Growth: Slow Recovery with Long-Term Potential

Turkey's real GDP growth in 2023 was relatively strong, at 5.1%, driven by strong domestic demand and a surge in private consumption. However, the IMF's projections show a slowdown in growth in 2024, with a forecast of 3.0%. This deceleration reflects the impact of tightening monetary conditions, lower credit growth, and fiscal consolidation efforts designed to bring inflation under control.

The medium-term outlook, however, is more optimistic. The IMF anticipates that Turkey will experience a growth rebound starting in 2025, with growth expected to reach 2.7%, gradually increasing towards 4% in the medium term. This growth will be supported by structural reforms aimed at improving productivity and diversifying the economy away from high-inflation and financial instability-driven growth. Despite this recovery, the projected growth rates remain below Turkey's historical averages, reflecting the structural challenges that the economy faces due to prolonged inflation and financial distortions.

In the longer term, Turkey's potential GDP growth remains relatively robust. Reforms, particularly those aimed at reducing informality in the labor market, improving energy efficiency, and modernizing the industrial base, could gradually push the economy closer to its pre-crisis growth trajectory. Nonetheless, the medium-term outlook remains subject to volatility, both due to global economic conditions and internal political and geopolitical risks.

Inflation Trajectory: A Slow and Steady Decline

Turkey's most pressing challenge in 2023 was hyperinflation, which peaked at over 72% mid-year before easing slightly in the latter part of the year. The IMF's forecast shows inflation at 52% by August 2024, but with a further decline expected, reaching 24% by the end of 2025.

The reduction in inflation is expected to be gradual due to the continuation of tight monetary policy, which includes high policy interest rates to bring real rates into positive territory. A more contractionary fiscal stance is also expected to ease domestic demand pressures, further helping to anchor inflation expectations. However, inflation risks remain as Turkey's economy faces strong inflation inertia, particularly from wage-driven inflation and past price increases that persist in the economy.

The central bank's goal of achieving a more stable and predictable inflation rate aligns with the IMF's expectation that inflation will not fall to target levels in the short term. Despite expectations for gradual disinflation, the high inflation rates will continue to impact the cost of living and erode purchasing power, especially for lower-income households.

Public Debt: A Managing Act in a Volatile Environment

Public debt in Turkey has been relatively well-managed, with gross debt falling from 40.4% of GDP in 2021 to 29.3% in 2023, aided by inflation, which eroded the real value of debt. However, the debt structure is a mixed picture. While overall debt levels remain relatively low compared to other emerging markets, the proportion of foreign-currency denominated debt exposes Turkey to exchange rate risks. As the lira depreciates or faces volatility, the cost of servicing foreign debt rises, which could put pressure on public finances.

Furthermore, the average cost of new domestic debt has surged from 10% in early 2023 to a high of 36% in June 2024, reflecting the increase in interest rates. While this increase does not yet significantly affect the overall fiscal balance, higher borrowing costs could exacerbate fiscal pressures if rates remain high for an extended period. Moreover, Turkey's fiscal position remains vulnerable to contingent liabilities arising from public-private partnerships (PPPs), losses at state-owned enterprises (SOEs), and potential pension reform costs. These liabilities, while not fully accounted for in the official debt numbers, represent substantial financial risks.

Looking ahead, the IMF has noted that fiscal consolidation efforts will need to be stepped up in order to maintain fiscal health. Public debt is projected to stabilize at 25-26% of GDP in the medium term, but Turkey will face challenges in managing its debt if inflation does not fall significantly, or if the global economic environment becomes less favorable.

Fiscal Deficit: Risks of Expansionary Policies

Turkey's fiscal deficit remains a key concern. Despite significant progress in fiscal consolidation in recent years, the budget deficit was projected at 5.2% of GDP in 2023, and the government's fiscal position remains under strain in

2024. The IMF projects a further decline in the fiscal deficit to 3.6% by 2025, supported by a combination of higher taxes and fiscal restraint. However, this forecast assumes that fiscal policies will remain consistent, with a focus on reducing non-essential government spending and curbing public sector wage increases.

The key challenge for Turkey's fiscal policy will be balancing austerity measures with the need for post-earthquake reconstruction spending. In 2023, earthquake-related expenditures were substantial, representing 7% of GDP, with over half of the spending allocated to rebuilding housing stock and supporting vulnerable populations. While earthquake reconstruction spending is expected to decline in 2024, the continued need for fiscal support will keep the deficit elevated in the short term. The IMF has emphasized the importance of maintaining fiscal discipline and further curbing unnecessary capital spending in order to avoid exacerbating fiscal imbalances.

Key Risks and Challenges

While Turkey's economic outlook is improving, several risks and challenges remain that could derail its recovery and growth trajectory:

Inflationary Inertia: While inflation is expected to decline gradually, Turkey faces significant risks from wage-driven inflation and price inertia. The continuation of minimum wage hikes and the potential for a resurgence in inflationary expectations pose a challenge to the central bank's ability to meet inflation targets.

Public Debt Management: As Turkey remains exposed to foreign currency debt, a sharp depreciation of the lira or a sudden spike in global interest rates could worsen Turkey's debt servicing burden. Although Turkey's overall debt remains manageable, external shocks could have disproportionate effects on the budget.

Geopolitical Risks: Turkey's geopolitical position in the Middle East, combined with its close ties to both the West and Russia, exposes the country to external shocks, such as geopolitical tensions or global commodity price fluctuations. Any escalation in regional conflicts could impact Turkey's economic stability, particularly if energy prices rise unexpectedly.

Structural Reform Challenges: While Turkey has embarked on significant economic reforms, particularly in the financial sector and monetary policy, there is a need for further structural reforms. Labor market inefficiencies, an overreliance on certain industries (e.g., construction), and the informal economy continue to undermine Turkey's long-term growth potential. The pace and effectiveness of these reforms will be critical to sustaining Turkey's recovery.

Conclusion: Turkey's Economic Prospects and Strategic Opportunities

Turkey's economy is slowly recovering, but significant challenges remain. The IMF's projections suggest that while growth will resume in 2025, it will be at a subdued pace, constrained by ongoing inflation pressures, fiscal deficits, and public debt vulnerabilities. However, Turkey's ongoing policy reforms, the gradual decline in inflation, and the government's focus on infrastructure investment present opportunities for those willing to navigate the economic challenges.

Investors should be aware of the risks associated with Turkey's high inflation, fiscal pressures, and external vulnerabilities, but they should also recognize the potential for long-term growth if structural reforms take hold and Turkey's economic fundamentals stabilize. The coming years will be a test of Turkey's ability to manage its debt, reduce inflation, and foster a more sustainable growth trajectory in a complex and ever-changing global landscape.

Bahaa G. Arnouk

Chapter (17)

Netherlands: A Strategic Economic and Investment Landscape Amid Transition

The Dutch economy, resilient yet facing critical crossroads, has shown flexibility in recent years, especially during the pandemic. Today, the Netherlands balances emerging economic opportunities with distinct challenges across inflation, climate policy, and fiscal sustainability. With insights from the IMF's 2024 Article IV consultation, the following overview explores the Netherlands' economic trajectory and investment potential amid its transformative policies in fiscal management, green technology, and digital advancement.

Steady Economic Recovery and Inflation Challenges

In 2023, the Netherlands experienced a cooling of economic growth to a minimal 0.1%, primarily due to higher energy costs, tight financial conditions, and reduced demand from key trading partners, notably Germany. Nevertheless, signs of resilience persist, and projections for 2024 suggest a modest growth uptick. Key economic dynamics include:

Inflation Dynamics: Core inflation remains above target, although it declined notably by December 2023 due to diminishing energy price shocks. While headline inflation is anticipated to ease to around 2.7% in 2024, the persistence of core inflation risks could necessitate prudent fiscal policies to prevent second-round inflationary effects from wage increases.

Labor Market Robustness: Despite cooling, the labor market continues to be tight, with high participation rates and low unemployment levels. This structural shortage underscores the importance of reforms in labor policies, particularly in enhancing productivity through technological adoption and skills development.

Fiscal Policies: Balancing Expansion and Sustainability

Fiscal policy in the Netherlands has been cautiously expansionary, yet future spending pressures call for strategic adjustments to maintain sustainability. The IMF's recommendations underscore the following:

Debt Stability and Structural Adjustments: While the Netherlands' public debt ratio remains modest compared to peers, long-term spending projections in healthcare, pensions, and defence will likely necessitate adjustments. The IMF suggests a phased deficit reduction averaging 0.3% of GDP yearly until 2028, achieved through prudent tax and spending reforms.

Streamlining Energy Subsidies: Efforts to phase out untargeted energy subsidies align with the Netherlands' environmental commitments while balancing fiscal sustainability. With recent cuts to implicit fossil fuel subsidies, fiscal resources can be reallocated towards targeted social programs, such as energy relief for vulnerable households.

Green and Digital Transitions: Investment in Sustainability and Innovation

The Netherlands has ambitious goals in green and digital transformations, setting the stage for strategic investment across green energy, digital infrastructure, and sustainable urban planning.

Climate and Energy Initiatives: As the Netherlands pursues a 60% reduction in greenhouse gases by 2030, the focus has shifted to a combination of lower subsidies, targeted carbon pricing, and stricter emissions standards. For investors, the nation's commitment to clean energy technology, especially in solar and electric vehicle infrastructure, presents unique opportunities in renewable energy markets and green tech sectors.

Digitalization Strategy: The Netherlands' digital transition is vital to alleviating labor shortages and enhancing economic productivity. Investments in digital infrastructure, including 5G and automation, have been prioritized. This push aims to foster a tech-driven economy that appeals to both local and international investors.

Financial Sector Stability and Housing Market Adjustments

The Dutch financial sector remains robust, yet heightened risks, particularly in the real estate market, warrant continued oversight. The IMF report highlights the following areas:

Banking Resilience: Dutch banks are well-capitalized, with strong liquidity and profitability metrics, yet real estate exposures are high. The financial system's sensitivity to real estate corrections could be mitigated through further adjustments in macroprudential policies and continued monitoring of mortgage lending standards.

Housing Market and Affordability: With an ongoing housing shortage, policies aim to balance affordability with stability. The IMF encourages gradual reductions in mortgage loan-to-value (LTV) ratios, tax reforms, and incentives to increase housing supply, which can also enhance economic stability by supporting a balanced real estate sector.

Strategic Sectors for Investment: Opportunities in Green Tech, Digital, and Healthcare

The Dutch economy's investment landscape is diversified and future-ready, particularly in the areas of:

Renewable Energy and Green Technologies: Policies incentivizing investments in green technology—such as subsidies for solar, wind, and energy storage—support the Netherlands' path toward sustainability. Investors targeting the renewable energy sector may benefit from the Netherlands' extensive policies supporting climate resilience.

Digital Infrastructure and Automation: Investments in digital transformation are integral to the Netherlands' economic agenda, aiming to enhance efficiency and reduce labor shortages. Digital advancements in AI, cybersecurity, and automated systems offer profitable pathways for investors interested in tech and digitalization.

Healthcare Innovation: As the Dutch population ages, demand in healthcare services, biotechnology, and telemedicine solutions grows. Investment in health technologies and elderly care innovation is likely to remain a high-value sector, supported by policy frameworks aimed at sustainable healthcare spending.

Key Takeaways for Investors

The Netherlands offers an evolving economic landscape where sustainability and innovation are key drivers of growth. However, investors should remain mindful of fiscal pressures and policy shifts that accompany this transformation. Strategic investment insights include:

Focus on Policy-Aligned Sectors: Investments in sectors receiving government support, such as green technology, digital infrastructure, and healthcare, are likely to benefit from stability and policy incentives.

Long-Term Vision for Sustainable Growth: The Netherlands' economic strategies, including its focus on climate and digitalization, align well with global Environmental, Social, and Governance (ESG) trends, which increasingly influence investment value. Sustainable and diversified portfolios in these areas are well-positioned for resilient returns.

Caution in Financial and Real Estate Investments: Given the heightened risk in the real estate sector, cautious investment strategies are advised. Monitoring of financial sector policies, particularly in macroprudential regulation, will be essential to navigate risks.

The Netherlands' Path Forward: An Era of Resilience and Innovation

The Netherlands' economic landscape reflects a commitment to sustainability, technological advancement, and fiscal discipline. As the IMF report indicates, the country's strategic focus on innovation and resilience presents a promising investment horizon. For forward-looking investors, the Netherlands provides a stable yet dynamic environment rich with opportunities across green, digital, and healthcare sectors, aligned with the global push for sustainable economic development.

Bahaa G. Arnouk

Chapter (18)

Saudi Arabia: A Thriving Economic Landscape Driving Global Investment Amid Transformation

Saudi Arabia is embarking on one of the most exhilarating economic transformations in the world. Under the visionary framework of Vision 2030, the Kingdom is revolutionizing its economy by diversifying away from oil dependence, fostering a robust non-oil sector, and positioning itself as a global leader in innovation and sustainability. The 2024 Article IV Consultation report from the International Monetary Fund (IMF) provides a powerful snapshot of Saudi Arabia's economic performance, fiscal policies, and strategic reforms, shedding light on the incredible opportunities available for investors eager to tap into this dynamic and fast-evolving market.

Economic Growth and Diversification: A Resilient and Expanding Economy

Despite the challenging headwinds of reduced oil production and global energy fluctuations, Saudi Arabia's economy remains remarkably resilient. In 2023, the Kingdom experienced a slight contraction in overall GDP of 0.8%, primarily driven by a deliberate cut in oil production under OPEC+ agreements. However, non-oil GDP surged by an impressive 3.8%, fuelled by strong private consumption and investment. This exceptional non-oil growth underlines the Kingdom's strategic shift towards a more diversified and sustainable economic model.

Looking ahead, Saudi Arabia's growth trajectory is poised to accelerate. While non-oil growth is expected to moderate slightly in 2024 to 3.5%, the IMF predicts a sharp rebound in 2025, with overall growth reaching an estimated 4.7% as oil production cuts ease. Over the next decade, the Kingdom's non-oil economy is projected to sustain an average growth rate of 3.7% annually, driven by investments in high-priority sectors like technology, tourism, and infrastructure. These sectors, supported by robust public investments and Vision 2030 initiatives, are accelerating the Kingdom's shift from oil to a thriving, diversified economy.

Saudi Arabia's private sector is now a driving force behind the country's economic momentum, with foreign direct investment (FDI) steadily increasing as the Kingdom's business environment becomes more competitive and globally integrated. The International Monetary Fund highlights that the nation's growth potential remains exceptional, with non-oil sectors like entertainment, finance, and real estate poised for extraordinary expansion.

Fiscal Policy: Ambitious Reforms and Sustainable Growth

Saudi Arabia is meticulously navigating its fiscal landscape to support long-term growth while maintaining stability. After posting a surplus in 2022, the Kingdom's fiscal balance shifted to a deficit in 2023, largely driven by a 12% fall in oil revenues due to voluntary production cuts and a dip in global oil prices. The IMF forecasts that Saudi Arabia's fiscal deficit will average 3% of GDP from 2024 to 2029, with public debt rising gradually from 26.2% of GDP in 2023 to 30% by 2025. This increase in debt is not a cause for concern—on the contrary, it reflects prudent borrowing to fund strategic investments in key sectors under Vision 2030.

The Saudi government has already embarked on a bold path of fiscal consolidation, focusing on enhancing non-oil revenue through tax reforms. With the introduction of VAT and ongoing improvements in tax administration, the country has seen a significant rise in non-oil revenues, which now contribute more than double the amount they did just a few years ago. However, further fiscal reforms, including the implementation of property taxes and personal income taxes, will be crucial to closing any remaining revenue gaps and ensuring the Kingdom's fiscal resilience in the face of declining oil revenues.

In addition to revenue reforms, the IMF stresses the importance of fiscal discipline. Saudi Arabia's fiscal strategy includes significant efforts to rationalize spending, particularly on subsidies and wages, while ensuring that investment spending is carefully targeted to maximize economic returns. The development of a Sovereign Asset-

Liability Management (SALM) framework is a critical step toward ensuring that the Kingdom's wealth is managed efficiently and that fiscal policies are aligned with long-term growth objectives.

Public Debt and Financial Management: Strengthening Fiscal Buffers

Saudi Arabia's public debt remains relatively low by international standards. In 2023, public debt stood at 26.2% of GDP and is expected to rise to 30% by 2025. This manageable level of debt is paired with robust fiscal buffers, supported by a sovereign wealth fund (PIF) that holds assets totalling $925 billion. The Kingdom's financial strategy focuses on ensuring that these buffers remain strong even as public debt increases. By leveraging foreign borrowings and strategically investing in high-impact sectors, Saudi Arabia is securing its economic future while diversifying its sources of revenue away from oil.

The IMF also emphasizes the need for careful management of contingent liabilities tied to large-scale projects, including those under public-private partnerships (PPP) and mega infrastructure developments. By maintaining a clear and transparent fiscal framework, the Kingdom is reducing the risks associated with these ventures while ensuring that investments contribute to long-term economic growth.

Inflation Control: Stable Prices Amid Rising Demand

Inflation in Saudi Arabia remains well under control, thanks to a credible exchange rate peg to the U.S. dollar and consistent domestic policies. In 2023, the average consumer price index (CPI) was 2.3%, and inflation is projected to ease to 1.9% in 2024. The IMF projects that inflation will stabilize around 2% in the medium term, supported by a steady supply of expatriate labor and rationalized energy subsidies.

However, certain sectors, particularly housing, are experiencing price pressures. Rental inflation has surged by 10.5% in major cities like Riyadh and Jeddah, driven by a significant influx of expatriate workers and the government's large-scale urban redevelopment projects. To address these pressures, the Saudi government has taken proactive measures to reduce energy subsidies and implement targeted social support programs for vulnerable populations. This balanced approach ensures that inflationary pressures remain contained, while also protecting the most affected segments of the population.

Investment Opportunities: A New Era of Growth

Saudi Arabia's Vision 2030 is a blueprint for transformation, creating a wealth of investment opportunities across a range of sectors. The IMF report highlights several key areas where investors can tap into the Kingdom's immense growth potential:

Infrastructure and Real Estate: The government's focus on mega-projects, such as NEOM, Qiddiya, and Red Sea

Global, is transforming the Kingdom's urban and tourism landscapes. These projects not only offer significant returns but also create long-term growth prospects in the real estate, hospitality, and construction sectors.

Tourism and Entertainment: Saudi Arabia's tourism industry is experiencing a renaissance, with net tourism income surging by 38% in 2023. The Kingdom's ambitious plans to host the 2030 World Expo and the 2029 Asian Winter Games will further fuel growth in hospitality, entertainment, and retail, creating ample investment opportunities in these dynamic sectors.

Renewable Energy and Green Technologies: Saudi Arabia is rapidly shifting towards renewable energy, investing heavily in solar, wind, and green technologies. This transition opens lucrative opportunities for investors in the clean energy space, particularly as the Kingdom strives to meet its net-zero emissions targets by 2060.

Technology and Digitalization: With a strong push towards digitalization, Saudi Arabia is fostering innovation in sectors such as fintech, artificial intelligence, and cybersecurity. As the Kingdom moves towards becoming a digital hub for the region, investors have a unique opportunity to participate in the development of cutting-edge technologies and smart city initiatives.

Key Takeaways for Investors: Seizing the Future

Saudi Arabia's economic transformation presents an exhilarating opportunity for investors, particularly those aligned with the Kingdom's Vision 2030 reform agenda.

However, to capitalize on these opportunities, investors should keep the following considerations in mind:

Fiscal and Debt Management: While public debt is on the rise, it remains well below international thresholds. Investors should keep an eye on fiscal reforms and debt management strategies, which will play a crucial role in maintaining long-term economic stability.

Vision 2030 Alignment: Investing in sectors that are central to Vision 2030—such as infrastructure, tourism, renewable energy, and digital technologies—offers significant potential for growth and returns.

Inflation and Price Pressures: While inflation is under control, rental prices and energy subsidy reforms are areas of focus. Sectors tied to real estate and infrastructure will benefit from the government's ongoing investments, while also being mindful of these inflationary dynamics.

Saudi Arabia: a beacon of growth and innovation

Saudi Arabia's economic landscape is entering a new era of growth and innovation, with immense potential for forward-thinking investors. From sustainable energy to tourism, real estate, and technology, the Kingdom is crafting an investment-friendly environment that promises long-term returns in an increasingly diversified and dynamic economy. For investors looking to engage with one of the world's most exciting economic transformations, Saudi Arabia offers unparalleled opportunities for growth, resilience, and strategic returns.

Chapter (19)

Switzerland: Navigating Economic Resilience with Strategic Investments Amidst Fiscal and Demographic Challenges

Switzerland stands as a pillar of economic stability and growth, but like many advanced economies, it faces a complex economic landscape shaped by both global uncertainties and domestic structural challenges. The IMF's 2024 report on Switzerland highlights a mixed picture: while the country is on a path to gradual economic recovery following a slowdown in 2023, significant fiscal pressures, demographic shifts, and geopolitical risks are looming large. This chapter delves deep into Switzerland's economic and investment landscape, leveraging the latest economic figures and the IMF's policy recommendations to outline key challenges and investment opportunities.

A Moderate Economic Recovery Amidst Global and Domestic Pressures

Switzerland's economy, after slowing to a growth rate of just 0.8% in 2023, is projected to rebound moderately with an estimated 1.3% growth in 2024, climbing to 1.4% in 2025.

This recovery is expected to be driven by a gradual improvement in external demand, easing financial conditions, and lower inflation pressures, which the Swiss National Bank (SNB) has effectively curbed through tightening measures. However, Switzerland's economy faces persistent headwinds, particularly from demographic trends and global geopolitical instability.

Key Economic Indicators:

Real GDP Growth: After a subdued growth of 0.8% in 2023, Swiss GDP is projected to grow at 1.3% in 2024, a modest recovery after the sharp slowdown caused by the war in Ukraine and tighter financial conditions.

Unemployment Rate: Switzerland's labor market remains robust with an unemployment rate at 2.0% in 2023, slightly rising to 2.3% in 2024. The country's historically low unemployment levels reflect a resilient labor market despite ongoing skill shortages.

Inflation Trends: Inflation, which peaked at 2.8% in 2022, moderated significantly to 2.1% in 2023, and the IMF projects inflation to remain within the SNB's target range of 0-2%, averaging 1.5% in 2024. This decline is due to lower energy prices and reduced imported inflation pressures.

Public Debt, Fiscal Surplus, and the Long-Term Fiscal Trajectory

Switzerland's fiscal discipline remains a cornerstone of its economic policy. The country's public debt trajectory is relatively favorable compared to other European nations, largely due to the effective implementation of the "debt-brake" rule, which ensures fiscal stability by linking government spending to cyclically-adjusted revenues. However, as the IMF report indicates, long-term fiscal pressures are mounting, particularly due to defense spending, pension reforms, and climate change mitigation costs.

Public Debt and Deficit/Surplus Trends:

Public Debt: Switzerland's public debt stood at 38.3% of GDP in 2023, a level that remains low by international standards. This marks a significant improvement from the 56.9% of GDP in 2003 when the debt-brake rule was introduced. The IMF projects a continued decline in debt, reaching 36.7% of GDP by 2024, and 35.6% by 2025. However, while the debt ratio is manageable, the country faces increasing fiscal pressures in the medium to long term.

Fiscal Surplus: Switzerland is expected to maintain a fiscal surplus of 0.5% of GDP in 2024, down from 1.2% in 2023. This surplus is primarily driven by strong performance from cantonal and social security funds, with the federal government running a small deficit of -0.1% in 2023. Despite these surpluses, spending pressures in areas like national defence, healthcare, and pensions are expected to increase in the coming years, challenging the government's ability to maintain this surplus without significant reforms.

Fiscal Sustainability: The IMF emphasizes the need for Switzerland to tackle its rising public spending in the medium term, particularly in defense and pension systems. Spending on national defense, for example, is projected to rise to 1% of GDP by 2035, up from 0.7% in 2019. Demographic-related expenditures are expected to climb from 17.2% of GDP in 2023 to 18.8% by 2040 and 19.8% by 2060. This underscores the urgency for reforms to ensure long-term fiscal sustainability.

Long-Term Challenges in Public Finances:

Pension System Pressures: A key challenge for Switzerland's public finances is the pension system, where a recent referendum passed in March 2024 mandates a 13th monthly pension payment starting in 2026. This new mandate will require an additional CHF 4.2 billion (0.5% of GDP) annually to fund, placing additional strain on the federal budget. To address these funding gaps, the government has proposed a combination of measures, including raising VAT rates and increasing contributions to the pension system.

Climate Change Expenditures: Switzerland's ambitious climate goals will also put pressure on public finances. The revised CO2 Act, passed in March 2024, lays out emissions-reduction targets for 2025–2030, though the IMF notes that the measures may not be ambitious enough to meet long-term goals. This could lead to increased reliance on international emissions-reduction credits, further complicating the fiscal outlook.

Monetary Policy: Tightening and Strategic Rate Cuts

The Swiss National Bank (SNB) has been effective in maintaining inflation within its 0 2% target range, using a combination of interest rate hikes and interventions in the foreign exchange market. In March 2024, the SNB cut its policy rate by 25 basis points to 1.75%, signalling a more dovish stance after aggressive rate hikes in 2023. This rate cut, which came ahead of most major central banks, is designed to ensure that inflation does not fall too low while continuing to support economic recovery.

Monetary Policy Adjustments:

Interest Rates and Inflation Management: The SNB has taken a cautious approach to monetary policy, managing the inflationary pressures from both domestic and external sources. With inflation expected to remain within the target range, the IMF suggests that the SNB will continue to adjust rates based on incoming data and international monetary trends.

Swiss Franc and Foreign Exchange Interventions: The SNB's interventions in the foreign exchange market in 2023—amounting to CHF 133 billion—played a key role in stabilizing the franc, which appreciated by 6.4% in 2023. However, the franc's recent depreciation in early 2024 has provided the SNB with some room to ease financial conditions, which is expected to support economic recovery.

Financial Sector Stability: The Credit Suisse Saga and Real Estate Vulnerabilities

Switzerland's financial sector remains resilient, despite significant challenges, including the 2023 crisis involving Credit Suisse. The state-facilitated acquisition of Credit Suisse by UBS helped stabilize the financial markets and prevented systemic financial stress. However, vulnerabilities persist, particularly in the real estate sector.

Banking Sector Resilience:

Credit Suisse and UBS Acquisition: The merger of Credit Suisse and UBS, while stabilizing the financial system, has created challenges due to the size of the combined entity, which now holds assets equivalent to 180% of Swiss GDP. The IMF report highlights the risks associated with the "Too-Big-To-Fail" (TBTF) status of UBS, which could complicate future financial crises.

Real Estate Exposure: Both the banking sector and non-bank financial institutions (NBFIs) are highly exposed to the real estate market, with residential mortgage loans constituting 75% of total bank loans. This high exposure, coupled with rising household debt, presents significant risks to financial stability. While house prices have adjusted somewhat due to higher interest rates, the Swiss real estate market remains vulnerable to external shocks and internal market imbalances.

Demographic Shifts and Structural Reforms

Switzerland's economic growth faces long-term challenges due to its aging population and skill gaps in key sectors such as technology, healthcare, and finance. The IMF report stresses the need for structural reforms to address these challenges, focusing on increasing labor force participation from women, older workers, and immigrants.

Labor Market and Demographic Challenges:

Labor Force Participation: Despite high participation rates, there are increasing skill shortages, particularly in tech and engineering. Policies aimed at increasing the participation of women, older workers, and immigrants will be crucial to mitigating these shortages and sustaining growth.

Pension and Retirement Age Reforms: The country is also facing pressure on its pension system. The government is considering reforms such as increasing the retirement age and modifying the pension contribution structure to address funding gaps exacerbated by demographic trends.

Strategic Investment Opportunities

Despite these challenges, Switzerland offers several investment opportunities that are aligned with its policy priorities and economic trends. Key areas for investment include green energy, technology, healthcare, and real estate.

High-Growth Sectors for Investment:

Green Energy and Sustainability: With Switzerland committed to ambitious climate goals, investments in renewable energy, electric vehicles, and carbon reduction technologies will see long-term growth. The recently revised CO_2 Act and the potential introduction of carbon border adjustments create a favorable environment for green investment.

Technology and Innovation: Switzerland is making strides in the digital economy, with fintech and AI emerging as key sectors for growth. Government investments in digital infrastructure and innovation will continue to drive growth in these areas.

Healthcare and Life Sciences: The aging population creates opportunities for investment in healthcare, biotechnology, and life sciences. Switzerland's strong healthcare system and focus on technological innovation in health provide solid investment avenues.

Real Estate and Infrastructure: The residential real estate market remains robust, driven by population growth and strong demand. Commercial real estate faces challenges but may offer opportunities in key locations as the economy recovers.

Key Takeaways for Investors:

Focus on High-Growth Sectors: Green energy, technology, and healthcare are poised for significant long-term growth.

Monitor Fiscal and Demographic Trends: Pay attention to rising pension costs and defence spending, which will affect fiscal policy and investment opportunities.

Diversify Across Resilient Sectors: Real estate and infrastructure, particularly in key urban areas, remain attractive, despite some vulnerabilities.

Conclusion: Switzerland's Path to Sustainable Growth

Switzerland's economic outlook for 2024 reflects a gradual recovery supported by stable fiscal policies, prudent monetary management, and key structural reforms. While fiscal challenges related to defence, pensions, and climate change persist, the country's strong fundamentals, coupled with targeted investments in green energy, technology, and healthcare, present attractive opportunities for investors. By aligning investment strategies with the Swiss government's priorities and navigating the evolving economic landscape, investors can tap into long-term growth potential, even amidst the challenges posed by demographic and fiscal pressures.

Switzerland's combination of fiscal discipline, strong financial stability, and a focus on sustainability and innovation positions it as an investment destination for those prepared to navigate its evolving economic landscape.

Chapter (20)

Argentina: A Blueprint for Economic Stability and Investment Amid Challenges

Argentina's economic landscape in 2024 reflects a pivotal moment as the nation strives to stabilize its economy, recover from long-standing fiscal imbalances, and unlock growth potential. The IMF's recent consultation report provides a detailed roadmap for fiscal discipline, monetary policy evolution, and structural reforms. Despite significant hurdles such as inflation, exchange rate volatility, and political uncertainties, Argentina's decisive measures to restore stability offer new opportunities for investors. In this chapter, we will explore Argentina's economic outlook, fiscal strategies, and investment prospects while addressing the challenges it faces.

Economic Outlook: Balancing Recovery and Stability

Argentina's economy is navigating a period of contraction and cautious recovery, with GDP projected to decline by **3.5% in 2024**, reflecting sharp adjustments in demand and

activity. A turnaround is anticipated in the latter half of the
year as fiscal consolidation eases and real wages recover.

Real GDP Performance: A sharper-than-expected
contraction in Q1:2024, driven by reduced private
consumption and public investment, signals challenges.
However, improved agricultural production and stabilizing
consumer confidence hint at emerging recovery trends.

Inflation Trajectory: Inflation, while still elevated, has
improved significantly. Monthly inflation fell to **8.8% in
April 2024**, down from 25.5% in December 2023. Year-on-
year inflation is expected to converge to **140% by end-
2024** from 150% previously, with further declines over the
medium term as peso demand stabilizes.

Exchange Rate Adjustments: A phased easing of exchange
controls and a move toward a flexible exchange rate policy
are central to improving Argentina's external
competitiveness.

Fiscal Policy and Public Debt: A Focus on Sustainable Adjustment

Argentina has prioritized fiscal discipline as the cornerstone
of its economic stabilization plan, aiming for a primary
surplus of **1.7% of GDP in 2024** and achieving its first
consecutive monthly fiscal surpluses in 16 years.

Fiscal Deficit Trajectory: The fiscal adjustment planned for
2024 represents a 5 percentage points of GDP improvement,
two-thirds of which had been achieved by April. This

includes discretionary expenditure cuts and revenue enhancements.

Revenue Measures: Key reforms include raising personal income tax (PIT) revenues, rationalizing subsidies, and introducing temporary import-related taxes. Efforts to broaden the tax base and combat evasion are critical to sustaining fiscal improvements.

Public Debt Dynamics: Argentina's gross public debt remains high but manageable, supported by domestic debt restructuring and reduced rollover risks. A successful debt exchange extended the maturity of 40% of peso debt due in 2024 to 2025–28.

Structural Reforms: Paving the Way for Growth

To unlock its economic potential, Argentina is pursuing structural reforms aimed at enhancing competitiveness, labor market flexibility, and investment conditions.

Energy Sector: Adjustments to utility tariffs (electricity up 270% and gas up 600%) are improving cost recovery and reducing fiscal pressures. The government is also aligning prices to encourage private sector investment in hydrocarbon production and renewables.

Labor Market and Governance: Proposed labor reforms aim to increase flexibility and promote formal employment. The government is also enhancing transparency through better oversight of public funds and tackling corruption via strengthened anti-money laundering measures.

Regulatory Reforms: A streamlined regulatory framework seeks to foster competition and attract investment in strategic sectors such as mining, energy, and technology.

Macroeconomic Indicators: Key Metrics at a Glance

Primary Fiscal Balance: A surplus of 0.6% of GDP by Q1:2024, exceeding program targets by ARS 3,000 billion, driven by higher trade-related taxes and expenditure restraint.

Reserves: Net international reserves have improved significantly, rising from negative US$11.2 billion to US$0.3 billion by April 2024, supported by stronger trade balances and reduced financial outflows.

Inflation: Monthly headline inflation dropped sharply, with core inflation reaching its lowest since January 2023, reflecting strong fiscal anchors and controlled demand.

Deficit and Debt: The deficit is on a path to decline below 3% of GDP by 2026, contingent on continued reforms and expenditure management. Public debt sustainability remains a key focus of fiscal strategy.

Investment Horizons: Opportunities in Strategic Sectors

Despite challenges, Argentina presents attractive opportunities for investors in energy, agriculture, and infrastructure. The government's efforts to create a more market-oriented economy and improve regulatory predictability are expected to drive investment.

Energy: Expansion of natural gas pipelines and the reduction of energy subsidies are creating significant growth potential in the energy sector.

Agriculture: Recovery in agricultural exports, coupled with tariff reductions on inputs, positions Argentina as a strong player in global food markets.

Infrastructure Development: Urbanization and logistics demand create openings for investments in transportation and public-private partnerships.

Risks and Resilience: Navigating Uncertainty

While Argentina's policy reforms are a step in the right direction, risks such as global economic volatility, social unrest, and delays in legislative approval remain. The IMF emphasizes the importance of agile policymaking and broad political support to sustain the recovery.

Policy Coordination: Aligning fiscal and monetary policies is critical to maintaining stability and investor confidence.

External Risks: Dependence on commodity markets and international financing underscores the need for prudent economic planning.

Conclusion: Argentina's Path to Stability and Growth

Argentina's commitment to stabilization and reform offers a promising yet challenging roadmap for economic recovery and investment growth. While the road ahead requires careful navigation, the country's efforts to address macroeconomic imbalances, improve fiscal discipline, and attract investment signal a brighter future for its economy.

The IMF consultation underscores the need for sustained reforms, political consensus, and investment in strategic sectors to secure long-term stability. As Argentina transitions into this new phase, it presents a unique opportunity for investors to engage in one of South America's most dynamic markets.

Chapter (21)

The UAE's Financial System: A Rock of Stability in Uncertain Times

The United Arab Emirates (UAE) is rapidly emerging as a global economic powerhouse, driven by its ambitious diversification strategy and commitment to sustainable growth. This chapter draws insights from the International Monetary Fund's (IMF) June 2023 Article IV Consultation report, explores the UAE's economic landscape, highlighting both challenges and opportunities for investors.

Beyond Oil: A Diversification Success Story

While oil remains a significant contributor to the UAE's economy, the nation is successfully diversifying, with non-hydrocarbon GDP growth projected to reach 3.8% in 2023. This growth is driven by robust domestic activity, particularly in tourism, boosted by a strong rebound in tourism and activity related to the Dubai World Expo, and capital expenditure. The IMF projects continued non-hydrocarbon growth in the medium term, supported by the UAE's 2050 strategies, which focus on trade, digitalization, and green initiatives.

The manufacturing sector is also expected to grow significantly over the medium term with the expansion of hydrocarbon and non-hydrocarbon related industries.

A Hub for Innovation and Investment

The UAE is attracting significant foreign direct investment (FDI) due to its business-friendly reforms, strategic location, and world-class infrastructure. The nation is also emerging as a hub for innovation, with significant investments in digital and green technologies. These factors make the UAE an attractive destination for businesses seeking growth and expansion.

The IMF report highlights the UAE's success in attracting safe-haven inflows and conducting major Initial Public Offerings (IPOs) amidst increased global uncertainty.

Navigating the Fiscal Landscape

The IMF report acknowledges the UAE's strong fiscal position, with large surpluses projected in the coming years due to elevated oil prices. The general government fiscal balance is projected to average 3.8 percent of GDP over the medium term. The report also highlights the UAE's commitment to maintaining a prudent fiscal stance and its successful issuance of USD 7 billion in international and AED 9 billion in domestic bonds. However, the report also encourages the authorities to further solidify the fiscal position by:

Bahaa G. Arnouk

Maintaining a prudent fiscal stance: Avoiding procyclical spending and building fiscal buffers to enhance medium-term sustainability.

Broadening the revenue base: Continuing to enhance non-hydrocarbon revenue, including through the newly introduced corporate income tax, which is expected to improve the adjusted non-hydrocarbon primary deficit by 2.2 percentage points to 20.4 percent of non-hydrocarbon GDP over 2023-2027.

Improving expenditure efficiency: Gradually phasing out subsidies while strengthening social safety nets. The IMF suggests a growth-friendly and credible medium-term average annual consolidation of the non-hydrocarbon primary fiscal deficit of around 0.4 percent of non-hydrocarbon GDP.

These measures will ensure fiscal sustainability and support the UAE's long-term economic goals. The report also suggests further strengthening public finances by broadening the tax base, improving tax collection efficiency, containing expenditure growth, and gradually phasing out subsidies.

A Secure and Stable Financial System

The UAE's financial system is characterized by its stability and resilience. Banks are well-capitalized and liquid overall, and the central bank is actively monitoring financial stability risks. The IMF report notes the banking sector's improved profitability due to higher interest income and steady private credit growth. However, the report also acknowledges the persistence of some vulnerabilities, including exposures to

153

real estate. The IMF report encourages the authorities to
continue strengthening the financial sector by:

Strengthening macroprudential frameworks: Ensuring
effective supervision of digital innovation and fintech
activities. The IMF recommends continued close monitoring
of financial stability risks, especially given the high level of
nonperforming loans, tightening financial conditions, and
banks' exposures to the real estate sector.

**Implementing measures to strengthen the AML/CFT
framework**: Addressing remaining deficiencies identified by
the Financial Action Task Force. The IMF welcomes the
major efforts under the National AML/CFT Strategy and
Action Plan and encourages continued actions to further
strengthen the regulatory regime in line with the enhanced
monitoring under the Financial Action Task Force.

These steps will further enhance the UAE's financial
system's robustness and attractiveness to investors. The
report also suggests promoting the effective management of
legacy NPLs, further strengthening regulation and
supervision of the insurance sector, and carefully balancing
opportunities and risks associated with digital innovation in
the banking and payments sector.

Opportunities Amidst Transformation

The IMF report highlights specific areas ripe for investment
in the UAE:

Digitalization: The UAE is investing heavily in digital
infrastructure and technologies, creating opportunities for
businesses in e-commerce, fintech, and artificial intelligence.

The IMF highlights the potential of harnessing the benefits of AI and digitalization through investments in enabling infrastructure to support diversification and a smooth energy transition.

Green Initiatives: The UAE is committed to achieving net-zero emissions by 2050, with ambitious plans for renewable energy, green finance, and sustainable infrastructure. The report emphasizes the importance of a balanced approach to energy transition, scaling up investments in renewable and clean energy while "greening" extraction processes.

Trade and Tourism: The UAE is expanding its trade partnerships and developing world-class tourism destinations, creating opportunities for businesses in logistics, hospitality, and related sectors. The IMF welcomes the UAE's advancement on Comprehensive Economic Partnership Agreements (CEPAs), which are expected to boost trade and integration in global value chains and further attract FDI.

Key Takeaways for Investors

Strategic Partnerships: Collaborating with local partners to navigate the regulatory environment and leverage their expertise.

Long-Term Vision: Focusing on projects aligned with the UAE's 2050 strategies, particularly those supporting economic diversification, private sector growth, and sustainability.

Due Diligence: Thoroughly assessing potential risks and opportunities, particularly those related to global economic shifts and the energy transition. The IMF report acknowledges the significant global uncertainties surrounding the UAE's outlook, including weaker growth, tighter financial conditions, and geopolitical developments.

A Beacon of Economic Progress

The UAE's economic transformation is a testament to its visionary leadership and commitment to sustainable development. The IMF report provides valuable insights for investors seeking to capitalize on the UAE's potential. With careful planning, strategic partnerships, and a long-term vision, investors can contribute to the UAE's continued economic success while reaping the rewards of its dynamic and growing market.

Chapter (22)

Austria: A Strategic Economic and Investment Landscape Amidst Transition

Austria, a country known for its economic resilience and robust social systems, is navigating through an evolving economic environment marked by post-pandemic recovery, fiscal reforms, inflationary pressures, and the imperative to meet ambitious green transition goals. The IMF's 2024 Article IV Consultation report sheds light on Austria's economic and fiscal trajectory, offering insights into the country's growth prospects, fiscal sustainability, and strategic investment sectors. As Austria faces both challenges and opportunities, understanding its current economic landscape and key policy directions is essential for investors looking for stable yet dynamic growth prospects.

Economic Recovery and Inflation Dynamics

Austria's economy demonstrated impressive recovery from the pandemic's initial shock, returning to pre-pandemic output levels by 2022. However, in 2023, a combination of high energy prices, inflationary pressures, and elevated interest rates resulted in a contraction of 0.8% in GDP.

Despite this downturn, Austria's economy is poised for a modest recovery in 2024, underpinned by private consumption driven by rising real wages. Key aspects shaping the economic outlook include inflation, labor market developments, and the broader macroeconomic environment.

Inflation Trajectory: A Gradual Decline

Austria's inflation has been persistently higher than the euro-area average, with core inflation proving particularly sticky due to rapid wage growth in the services sector. The sharp spike in inflation to nearly 12% in early 2023 was driven by soaring energy prices exacerbated by the geopolitical tensions surrounding Russia's invasion of Ukraine. Since then, inflation has gradually moderated, with energy prices stabilizing, but core inflation has remained above 4% as services, particularly in tourism and hospitality, continued to experience upward price pressures.

Inflation Projections: The IMF anticipates a gradual reduction in inflation, with headline inflation expected to ease to around 4.0% in 2024, eventually reaching the European Central Bank's 2% target by the second half of 2025. However, the persistence of high services sector inflation means that Austria may not see a full return to price stability for some time. Investors should be mindful of inflation risks in sectors with sticky price levels, especially in consumer services and real estate.

Labor Market Resilience Amidst Economic Contraction

Despite economic contraction, Austria's labor market remains resilient, reflecting tight employment conditions and significant wage growth. In 2023, Austria's employment rate reached record highs, and wages grew faster than the euro-area average. However, the economic slowdown has led to a slight increase in unemployment and a decrease in vacancy rates. Structural shifts are also visible, particularly in the growing share of part-time employment, reflecting evolving work preferences.

Key Labor Market Trends: The trend toward more part-time and flexible work arrangements, particularly among women, reflects broader societal changes. The IMF report highlights the need for continued labor market reforms to address demographic pressures, such as increasing the labor participation rate of elderly workers and closing gender wage gaps. The shift towards part-time employment and a reduction in total hours worked suggest potential challenges in labor productivity and economic growth, particularly as Austria faces an aging population.

Fiscal Policies: Balancing Sustainability with Strategic Investments

Austria's fiscal policy has played a critical role in mitigating recent economic shocks, but significant challenges remain. While the fiscal deficit narrowed slightly to 2.7% of GDP in 2023, fiscal pressures are mounting due to demographic trends, rising healthcare costs, and defense spending needs. The IMF report highlights the importance of continued fiscal consolidation to stabilize public debt while ensuring sufficient room for strategic investments, particularly in green infrastructure.

Public Debt and Deficit: Managing Long-Term Sustainability

Austria's public debt ratio, while still relatively low compared to other European nations, increased to 77.7% of GDP in 2023, largely due to pandemic-related spending and energy-price support measures. The IMF projects a gradual reduction in the debt-to-GDP ratio over the medium term, but demographic factors, including the aging population and rising social welfare costs, are expected to exert upward pressure on public spending.

Fiscal Deficit Reduction: The IMF advocates for a cautious approach to deficit reduction, suggesting a moderate fiscal tightening of 0.3% of GDP annually through 2028 to bring the structural primary balance close to zero by 2028. This would stabilize the public debt at sustainable levels and allow room for investment in green infrastructure and other critical areas. The government has already begun phasing out energy subsidies, which will help reduce the fiscal deficit, though higher public investment in climate initiatives and defense could offset these savings.

Green Transition Investment Needs

Austria is committed to achieving a 48% reduction in non-ETS emissions by 2030, but the current trajectory falls short of this target. The country has made progress in integrating renewable energy sources, but regulatory delays in green project approvals and skill shortages in key sectors pose significant challenges.

Investment Opportunities in Green Infrastructure: The IMF emphasizes that accelerating the green transition will require substantial public investment in renewable energy infrastructure, energy efficiency, and green technologies. Public-private partnerships, particularly in the energy sector, offer significant opportunities for investors in clean energy, energy storage solutions, and sustainable urban infrastructure.

Inflation and Monetary Policy: Adjusting to Changing Conditions

Austria's inflation dynamics remain a critical factor in shaping its economic policies. While the country is expected to see a reduction in inflation in the coming years, the pace of this decline will depend on global energy prices, domestic wage pressures, and the overall economic environment in the Eurozone.

Monetary Policy Outlook: The IMF anticipates that the European Central Bank's monetary easing in 2024–2025 will help bolster investment demand, although the persistent inflationary pressures, particularly in services, could necessitate a prolonged period of cautious monetary policy. For investors, this environment suggests a need to closely monitor ECB actions, particularly in terms of interest rates and their impact on credit availability.

Investment Opportunities: Green Energy, Digital Infrastructure, and Housing

Austria's investment landscape is diverse, with significant opportunities in sectors aligned with its long-term growth strategy, such as green energy, digital infrastructure, and housing. The country's green transition goals, combined with its commitment to digitalization, make it a prime location for strategic investments.

Green Energy Transition: A High-Value Investment Sector

Austria's ambitious environmental goals—such as achieving net-zero emissions by 2040 and reducing emissions by 48% by 2030—are driving investment in renewable energy and energy efficiency. Investment in solar, wind, and energy storage technologies is crucial to meet these targets.

Government Support for Green Initiatives: The IMF report highlights the importance of removing regulatory bottlenecks and enhancing public investment in green infrastructure. Investors in clean energy, particularly in solar, wind, and electric vehicle infrastructure, are likely to benefit from Austria's green transition policies and EU-backed funding mechanisms aimed at reducing carbon emissions.

Digitalization and Innovation: A Key Growth Driver

Austria's commitment to digitalizing its economy is another important area for investment. The country has outlined strategic plans to improve digital connectivity, particularly in rural areas, and to support the adoption of automation technologies. Investment in digital infrastructure, including

162

5G, AI, and cybersecurity, presents long-term opportunities for growth.

Investing in Digital Infrastructure: The IMF emphasizes the need for continued investment in digital infrastructure to improve economic productivity and mitigate labor shortages. Investors in tech and digital infrastructure will find fertile ground in Austria as the government accelerates digital adoption across sectors.

Real Estate and Housing Market Challenges

The Austrian housing market, particularly in Vienna, faces significant affordability challenges. With real house prices increasing by 74% from 2010 to 2021, the supply of new housing has not kept up with demand. Strict regulatory controls and permitting delays have contributed to housing market bottlenecks.

Investment in Housing and Urban Development: Austria's government is taking steps to ease restrictions on new housing construction and improve housing affordability. Investment in residential real estate and urban development, particularly in Vienna and other urban centers, presents opportunities as regulatory constraints ease and new housing projects move forward.

Key Takeaways for Investors

Austria offers a promising yet complex investment landscape. The country's commitment to sustainability, technological innovation, and fiscal discipline creates a favorable environment for long-term growth. However, there are several key factors that investors should consider:

Policy-Aligned Investment Sectors: Investors in green technology, digital infrastructure, and renewable energy will benefit from government support and EU funding, which are critical to Austria's long-term growth.

Fiscal Sustainability and Structural Reforms: While Austria has room for fiscal flexibility, careful management of public debt and strategic spending cuts will be essential in maintaining long-term fiscal sustainability.

Caution in Housing and Real Estate: Given the high overvaluation of housing, particularly in Vienna, investors should be cautious in the real estate sector. Monitoring regulatory changes and housing supply improvements will be crucial for navigating potential market corrections.

Austria's Path Forward: Strategic Growth Amid Challenges

Austria is at a pivotal point in its economic journey. As it works to manage demographic challenges, reduce inflationary pressures, and meet its green transition goals, the country remains a key player in Europe's economic landscape. For investors, Austria offers a dynamic and stable environment, with opportunities across green energy, digital infrastructure, and sustainable housing. By aligning investments with Austria's long-term policy goals, investors can position themselves for success in one of Europe's most promising markets.

Chapter (23)

Singapore's Economic and Investment Landscape: Strategic Outlook for 2024 and Beyond

Singapore has long been recognized as a robust economic hub in Southeast Asia, driven by its open-market policies, strategic location, and strong financial sector. However, the global landscape in 2024 presents a mix of opportunities and challenges that could shape the country's economic trajectory in the years ahead. Following a moderate slowdown in 2023, Singapore is set to recover in 2024, but underlying risks related to inflation, fiscal sustainability, and an aging population will require careful navigation. The IMF 2024 Article IV Consultation Report offers a detailed analysis of Singapore's macroeconomic landscape, and this chapter delves deeper into its growth prospects, fiscal health, and investment opportunities, supported by key economic numbers and projections.

Economic Growth and the Path to Recovery

2023: A Year of Moderate Growth

Singapore's economy grew by 1.1% in 2023, a sharp decline from the 3.8% growth experienced in 2022. This moderation was primarily driven by a contraction in manufacturing, especially in electronics, a sector that had experienced a downturn due to global supply chain disruptions and declining demand in the semiconductor market. This decline in external demand for Singapore's electronics products significantly impacted non-oil domestic exports (NODX), which contracted by 10.1% in 2023. Despite these setbacks, Singapore showed signs of resilience, with private consumption and net exports helping to cushion the economic downturn.

However, by the second half of 2023, Singapore's economy began to recover. In the fourth quarter of 2023, GDP growth surged to 2.2% year-on-year, supported by a rebound in semiconductor demand and a recovery in tourism. This upward trend continued into 2024, with the first quarter of 2024 witnessing a growth rate of 2.7% year-on-year. The IMF forecasts 2.1% GDP growth for the full year, driven by a continuation of the tech cycle recovery, stronger global demand, and a rise in inbound tourism.

Economic Projections: A Gradual Recovery in 2024 and Beyond

For 2024, Singapore's growth trajectory is expected to be more balanced. The IMF projects that real GDP growth will recover to 2.1%, which will be underpinned by stronger external demand, especially from the semiconductor industry, and a modest rebound in the tourism sector. The IMF's projections suggest that Singapore will see growth reaching 2.7% in the first half of 2024, as the impact of the semiconductor cycle takes full effect.

Over the medium-term, Singapore's growth is expected to gradually converge towards 2.5% per year by 2025. The primary drivers of this steady growth will be an increase in private consumption, fueled by higher wages and strong employment, alongside capital accumulation and related improvements in total factor productivity. However, the aging population remains a significant headwind to faster economic growth, as the workforce shrinks, and dependency ratios rise.

Inflation and Monetary Policy: Navigating a Tight Environment

Disinflationary Pressures

Inflation has been one of the critical economic challenges for Singapore in recent years. After experiencing a sharp rise in 2022 (with CPI inflation reaching 6.1%), the country has witnessed a gradual moderation in inflationary pressures. By April 2024, headline inflation had eased to 2.7%, and the Monetary Authority of Singapore's (MAS) core inflation (which excludes accommodation and private transport) had declined to 3.1%.

The disinflationary trend is primarily supported by a decline in global energy prices and easing cost pressures in food and tradable goods. However, the services sector continues to face persistent inflationary pressures, especially in healthcare and food services, as accumulated cost pressures from the previous years affect consumer prices. The increase in the Goods and Services Tax (GST) to 9% in January 2024 is also expected to temporarily raise inflation before moderating later in the year.

MAS Monetary Stance

In response to persistent inflationary pressures, MAS has maintained a tight monetary policy stance. The MAS operates an exchange rate-based policy framework, which has kept the nominal effective exchange rate (S$NEER) on an appreciating path. The IMF's report indicates that the MAS has made significant adjustments since October 2021, raising the slope of the exchange rate band to keep imported inflation under control and support domestic price stability. Interest rates remained elevated throughout 2023, helping to cool down the housing market and moderate credit demand.

Looking ahead, the IMF suggests that tight monetary policy should remain in place until inflationary pressures firmly recede. With inflation expected to gradually moderate to 3% in 2024, the MAS will likely maintain its policy stance until the inflation rate approaches its target of around 2% by 2025.

Public Debt, Fiscal Deficit, and Long-Term Fiscal Sustainability

Fiscal Performance and Surplus

Singapore has maintained strong fiscal discipline, supported by a robust fiscal framework. In FY2023, the government recorded a surplus of 0.8% of GDP, driven largely by higher-than-expected corporate income tax collections. Despite the fiscal surplus in 2023, the government is mindful of future spending needs, particularly due to the rapidly aging population and growing healthcare costs.

In response to these long-term challenges, Singapore has increased its GST rates to 9% starting in January 2024, a move that is expected to generate additional revenue to cover rising public expenditures. The government has also increased its carbon tax from S$5 per tonne to S$25 per tonne in January 2024, which will provide additional resources for green initiatives and public investment.

The IMF's analysis highlights that Singapore is well-positioned to increase public spending over the medium term, owing to its strong fiscal institutions and substantial reserves. However, the report also suggests that fiscal policy should remain neutral in FY2024, with limited impacts on aggregate demand, while continuing to address higher living costs for vulnerable households.

Long-Term Fiscal Challenges

Looking further ahead, Singapore faces substantial fiscal challenges driven by demographic changes. The aging population will place increased pressure on healthcare and social security programs, with healthcare spending projected to rise from 4.2% of GDP in 2015 to 8.6% by 2050. The government has outlined plans to meet these rising costs, including increasing the GST rate and leveraging returns from its sovereign wealth funds like GIC and Temasek.

The IMF suggests that while Singapore has considerable fiscal flexibility in the short term, there will be a need for more gradual fiscal surplus accumulation in the coming years to accommodate these long-term spending needs without undermining fiscal sustainability.

Risks and External Vulnerabilities

External Economic Risks

While Singapore's economy is projected to recover, it remains vulnerable to several external risks, particularly from geopolitical tensions and shifts in global economic conditions. As a small, open economy, Singapore is highly exposed to fluctuations in global demand, especially from key trading partners like China and the U.S.. Any slowdown in the Chinese economy, which accounts for a significant portion of Singapore's exports, could pose risks to Singapore's growth. The ongoing global geopolitical tensions, including the possibility of heightened trade frictions and supply chain disruptions, also present significant downside risks.

Additionally, the IMF has noted that geoeconomic fragmentation — the increasing tendency of countries to adopt inward-facing policies — could disrupt Singapore's integration into global supply chains, especially in technology and manufacturing.

Risks from Inflation and Housing Market Volatility

Inflation risks remain tilted to the upside, particularly in the **services sector**, where cost pressures have persisted. Additionally, the rise in interest rates and mortgage costs could result in a cooling of the housing market, but the property sector still poses a potential risk, especially if commercial real estate prices decline further.

The tight macroprudential policies currently in place, including limits on loan-to-value ratios and debt-servicing ratios, aim to prevent systemic risks from emerging in the housing sector. However, the IMF advises that Singapore should remain vigilant against potential vulnerabilities, especially in light of rising housing prices and tight lending conditions.

Investment Opportunities in Singapore

Despite these challenges, Singapore remains a promising destination for investment, particularly in sectors aligned with the country's long-term growth and sustainability goals.

Green Infrastructure and Sustainability

With the government's commitment to achieving carbon neutrality by 2050, investment in green infrastructure is a key area of focus. The rise of green bonds, carbon taxes, and investments in renewable energy and climate resilience create substantial opportunities in the clean energy sector.

Digital Transformation and Innovation

Singapore's push toward digitalization offers significant opportunities in fintech, artificial intelligence (AI), and cybersecurity. The country's strong regulatory framework, coupled with initiatives to develop smart cities and digital financial services, makes it an attractive market for technology-focused investments.

Healthcare

As an aging population places increasing demands on Singapore's healthcare system, there are considerable investment opportunities in the healthcare sector. Investments in medical services, elderly care, and biotechnology are expected to grow as the government ramps up its healthcare expenditure.

Conclusion: A Resilient Yet Evolving Economic Landscape

Singapore's economic outlook for 2024 is cautiously optimistic, with gradual recovery from the pandemic-induced slowdown expected to continue through the year. However, investors need to remain cognizant of the challenges that lie ahead, particularly inflationary pressures, fiscal sustainability concerns, and risks from global economic shifts.

By aligning investments with Singapore's strategic policy goals, especially in green energy, digital innovation, and healthcare, investors can capitalize on the country's long-term growth trajectory. At the same time, they must carefully monitor external risks and the evolving fiscal landscape to ensure resilience in a dynamic and interconnected global economy.

Chapter (24)

Malaysia's Economic and Investment Landscape: In-Depth Strategic Outlook for future

Malaysia stands as a key player in Southeast Asia, with its economic resilience tested by both global disruptions and domestic challenges. In 2024, the country faces a more moderate growth path than its impressive recovery in 2022, but strong fundamentals, fiscal reforms, and an ambitious structural agenda continue to guide its economic trajectory. This chapter delves deeper into Malaysia's economic growth, inflationary dynamics, fiscal consolidation, public debt sustainability, and emerging investment opportunities. Drawing insights from the IMF's 2024 Article IV Consultation report, we'll explore the country's fiscal health and prospects for investors looking to capitalize on its evolving economic landscape.

Economic Growth: Slowing Momentum Amid Resilience

2023: Slower Growth, Driven by Domestic Demand

Malaysia's economy grew by 4% in 2023, a sharp slowdown from 8.7% in 2022. The contraction in export demand, particularly for electrical and electronics (E&E) products, was a key factor, as the global demand for these goods weakened significantly. Additionally, Malaysia faced external headwinds from global trade slowdowns, especially with its largest trading partner, China. Despite this, domestic consumption remained a key growth engine. The labor market showed resilience, with a decline in the unemployment rate to pre-pandemic levels of 3.3% by November 2023. Tourism recovery also provided a boost, underlining the importance of services in the post-pandemic recovery phase.

However, the IMF projects a slight acceleration in Malaysia's GDP growth to 4.3% in 2024. This is expected to be driven by continued private consumption, recovery in public investment, and a rebound in external demand for E&E products. While global headwinds will remain, particularly in China and other key markets, Malaysia's growth is forecast to stay positive due to resilient domestic drivers. Over the medium term, the economy is expected to stabilize at around 4.4% growth per year, supported by a combination of public and private investments, alongside a gradual recovery in exports.

Structural Reforms and Long-Term Growth

The IMF highlights that Malaysia's long-term growth trajectory will largely depend on its ability to implement significant structural reforms. Key areas for reform include improving labor market outcomes, enhancing governance, promoting digitalization, and addressing climate change. Achieving these reforms will be crucial to unlocking higher productivity, wage growth, and ultimately, the country's path to high-income status.

Inflation and Monetary Policy: Navigating Pressures

Inflation Outlook: Moderating, but Risks Remain

Malaysia's inflation trajectory in 2023 demonstrated a significant easing, with the Consumer Price Index (CPI) falling to 2.5% from 3.4% in 2022. The moderation was driven by a reduction in energy and food prices, while core inflation also dropped to 3% from 4.2% the previous year. However, inflationary pressures are expected to tick up slightly in 2024, with the IMF forecasting a rise to 2.9%, largely due to uncertainties around subsidy reforms and ongoing shifts in global commodity prices.

The Malaysian government's ongoing subsidy reform is a crucial factor influencing the inflation outlook. The IMF notes that Malaysia is gradually targeting subsidies more effectively, such as the reallocation of fuel subsidies towards lower-income households and public transport sectors. However, the implementation of these reforms is still evolving, with the impact on inflation expectations remaining uncertain.

Monetary Policy: Tighter Stance to Combat Inflation Risks

Bank Negara Malaysia (BNM) adopted a neutral monetary policy stance by maintaining the overnight policy rate (OPR) at 3.0% after a series of hikes in 2022 and early 2023. While inflation has moderated, the IMF suggests that BNM should retain a tightening bias until inflationary risks, particularly from subsidy reforms, are fully contained. The risks of higher inflation from a weaker ringgit and rising global commodity prices—especially oil—further support the case for cautious monetary policy.

The IMF's report emphasizes that BNM's approach will be crucial in stabilizing prices, and the central bank must remain vigilant to inflationary pressures, especially in the services sector. Given the uncertain trajectory of energy prices and the risk of second-round effects from subsidy reforms, the IMF suggests maintaining a flexible and data-dependent policy stance.

Fiscal Health: Consolidation and Debt Sustainability

Fiscal Deficit and Debt Projections

Malaysia's fiscal health remains a key concern as the government works towards deficit reduction. The IMF's report outlines the government's fiscal consolidation strategy, which targets reducing the overall fiscal deficit from 5% of GDP in 2023 to 4.3% in 2024. A primary driver of this reduction is the ongoing subsidy reform, which aims to reduce government spending on energy subsidies. While the 2023 budget met its deficit target, public spending has been relatively high due to continued subsidies and development expenditure.

The IMF's projections suggest that Malaysia's fiscal deficit will continue to narrow over the medium term, reaching below 3% by 2026. However, the IMF also stresses the need for Malaysia to adopt credible and durable revenue mobilization measures to maintain fiscal sustainability. Malaysia's reliance on volatile petroleum revenues poses risks to the long-term sustainability of public finances. As a result, the IMF recommends diversifying revenue sources, including the potential reintroduction of the Goods and Services Tax (GST), as a means of ensuring a more stable fiscal base.

Public Debt Sustainability: Risks and Strategies

Malaysia's public debt, which has remained above 60% of GDP, is another critical area of focus. The IMF estimates that the government's debt will stabilize at around 66.5% of GDP in the coming years. While this level is relatively manageable compared to other emerging economies, it remains elevated and underscores the need for fiscal reforms. To safeguard long-term debt sustainability, the IMF suggests that Malaysia should continue focusing on fiscal consolidation, leveraging its fiscal reforms, and generating higher tax revenues to prevent further debt accumulation.

The government's commitment to fiscal transparency, exemplified by the passage of the Public Finance and Fiscal Responsibility Act (FRA) in 2023, is a positive step towards ensuring greater fiscal accountability and long-term sustainability. The FRA mandates improved transparency in financial reporting and includes provisions for greater control over public sector liabilities, which could help mitigate fiscal risks in the future.

Risks and External Vulnerabilities

External Economic Risks

Malaysia's external position in 2023 was stronger than expected, but significant risks remain. The IMF notes that the global economic slowdown, particularly in China, presents a downside risk to Malaysia's growth. China's slowing demand for E&E products could weigh on Malaysia's export performance, while ongoing geopolitical tensions and commodity price volatility also pose risks. As a commodity exporter, Malaysia is vulnerable to fluctuations in global oil prices, which could affect fiscal revenue and economic growth.

In addition to these external risks, the IMF highlights concern over potential global inflationary shocks and interest rate hikes in major economies, which could lead to capital outflows and financial instability. Malaysia's exposure to external debt—estimated to be around 66% of GDP—further amplifies vulnerabilities in the face of rising global borrowing costs.

Domestic Risks: Political Uncertainty and Fiscal Pressures

On the domestic front, Malaysia faces risks from political instability, which could delay the implementation of key reforms. While the government is committed to advancing its economic agenda, ongoing political uncertainties could disrupt the reform momentum and hinder long-term growth prospects. Additionally, the IMF cautions that Malaysia's fiscal risks, particularly from contingent liabilities, remain elevated, requiring proactive management to ensure fiscal stability.

Investment Opportunities in Malaysia

Despite these challenges, Malaysia offers several promising investment opportunities, particularly in sectors aligned with the country's long-term growth strategies.

Green Energy and Sustainable Infrastructure

Malaysia is focusing on enhancing its sustainability credentials, with a particular emphasis on renewable energy sources like solar, hydro, and wind. The government's commitment to achieving carbon neutrality by 2050 presents long-term opportunities in green infrastructure, clean energy projects, and green bonds.

Digitalization and Technology

Malaysia's push toward digital transformation creates significant investment opportunities in sectors such as fintech, e-commerce, and artificial intelligence. With the government's strong support for technology adoption and digital infrastructure, investors can capitalize on the country's growing tech ecosystem, particularly in areas such as data centers and cybersecurity.

Tourism and Services Sector

With the rebound of global tourism, Malaysia's hospitality and tourism industries are set to experience growth. Investment in hotels, resorts, and related infrastructure, especially in key tourist destinations, is expected to yield returns as travel demand increases.

Healthcare and Aging Population

Malaysia's aging population presents opportunities in the healthcare sector, especially in elderly care, biotechnology, and medical services. The government's focus on improving healthcare infrastructure and services will drive investment in this sector.

Conclusion: Strategic Path Forward

Malaysia's economic outlook for 2024 remains cautiously optimistic, with growth expected to stabilize at around 4.3%. The country's efforts to address fiscal imbalances, diversify revenue sources, and reform key sectors will be critical in shaping its long-term economic trajectory. Investors looking to capitalize on Malaysia's growth story should focus on sectors aligned with the country's strategic goals, particularly green energy, digitalization, and healthcare.

While the country faces risks from global economic uncertainty and domestic political fragility, Malaysia's commitment to fiscal reform, economic diversification, and structural transformation offers a promising environment for long-term investment. By staying attuned to the evolving macroeconomic landscape and the government's reform efforts, investors can navigate the complexities of Malaysia's economy and capitalize on its growth potential in the years ahead.

Chapter (25)

Navigating Egypt's Economic Transformation: Challenges, Opportunities, and a Glimpse of Hope

Egypt's economic landscape is undergoing a significant transformation, navigating a challenging period while striving for a private-sector-led resurgence. This chapter draws insights from the International Monetary Fund's (IMF) July 2024 Staff Report for the Third Review under the Extended Fund Facility, offers a nuanced perspective on the challenges and opportunities in the Egyptian market.

Battling Headwinds, Seeking Stability

Egypt's recent economic performance has been subdued, with growth slowing to 2.7% in FY2023/24. This slowdown reflects a confluence of factors, including global headwinds, regional conflicts (particularly the conflict in Gaza and Israel), and domestic challenges such as high inflation. While inflationary pressures are gradually abating, reaching 27.5% in June 2024, they remain a key concern for policymakers.

The IMF report acknowledges these challenges but highlights positive developments stemming from the government's commitment to its reform program. The recent unification of the exchange rate and monetary policy tightening have brought greater stability to the foreign exchange market, attracting foreign inflows and bolstering investor confidence.

Fiscal Consolidation: A Balancing Act

Egypt faces a challenging fiscal landscape, with high public debt and significant financing needs. The government is pursuing a strategy of fiscal consolidation, targeting a primary surplus of 3.5% of GDP (excluding divestment proceeds) in FY2024/25. This effort involves a delicate balance between reducing debt and maintaining essential social spending.

Key elements of the fiscal strategy include:

Revenue Mobilization: The government is committed to a revenue-based consolidation, aiming to increase tax revenue by 3% of GDP over the program period. This includes plans for a comprehensive VAT reform, streamlining exemptions, and enhancing tax administration.

Subsidy Reform: A gradual reduction of untargeted fuel subsidies is planned, with a firm commitment to restore fuel prices to cost-recovery levels by December 2025. This will create fiscal space for more targeted social support measures.

Debt Management: An active debt management strategy is being pursued to reduce gross financing needs and debt. This includes extending the maturity of domestic debt issuance and exploring options like debt swaps.

Ras El-Hekma: A Beacon of Hope?

Overall, the Ras El-Hekma project represents a significant bet on Egypt's economic future, with the potential to transform a coastal region into a thriving economic hub. However, its success will depend on careful planning, effective execution, and the government's ability to manage associated risks.

Structural Reforms: A Long Road Ahead

The IMF report emphasizes the importance of structural reforms to unlock Egypt's long-term growth potential. Key areas for reform include:

State-Ownership Policy: Implementation of the State Ownership Policy is crucial to level the playing field for private businesses, reduce the state's economic footprint, and promote competition. This involves divestment of state-owned assets, strengthening corporate governance of SOEs, and enhancing transparency.

Business Environment: Improving the business climate is essential to attract investment and foster private sector growth. This includes streamlining regulations, enhancing trade facilitation, and strengthening the competition framework.

Financial Sector: Strengthening the financial sector is vital for supporting economic growth. This involves enhancing governance practices in state-owned banks, promoting competition, and ensuring financial stability.

Navigating the Waters: A Cautious Outlook.

The IMF report recommends a cautious outlook for Egypt's economy due to significant external and domestic risks. Regional conflicts and a potential global slowdown threaten external stability. Domestically, maintaining a flexible exchange rate, curbing inflation, and accelerating structural reforms are crucial. Fiscal risks from contingent liabilities and potential overheating from the Ras El-Hekma project require careful management. Sustained commitment to reforms and prudent policies are essential for a durable recovery.

Egypt's economic journey is fraught with challenges, but the government's commitment to its reform program offers a glimmer of hope. The IMF report provides a valuable roadmap for navigating this complex landscape.

Key takeaways for investors:

Assess Risk Carefully: While reforms are yielding positive results, Egypt faces significant risks, including regional conflicts, high inflation, and potential fiscal pressures. Investors should conduct thorough due diligence and consider these risks carefully.

Prioritize Sustainable Investment: The report highlights the importance of private-sector-led growth and economic diversification. Investors should prioritize projects aligned with these goals, particularly those contributing to sustainable development, job creation, and export potential.

Understand the Regulatory Landscape: Egypt's regulatory environment can be complex. Partnering with local entities with strong expertise and understanding of the legal and regulatory framework is crucial.

Engage with Reform Agenda: The success of Egypt's economic transformation hinges on the government's commitment to its reform agenda. Investors should engage with policymakers and advocate for continued progress on reforms that improve the business environment, enhance transparency, and level the playing field.

Monitor Macroeconomic Developments: Egypt's macroeconomic situation is evolving. Investors should closely monitor developments related to inflation, exchange rate policy, fiscal balances, and debt management, as these factors can significantly impact investment returns.

Egypt: A Glimmer of Hope Amidst Economic Headwinds

In essence, the IMF report suggests a cautious but engaged approach for investors in Egypt. Opportunities exist, but they require careful risk assessment, a focus on sustainability, and an understanding of the evolving policy landscape.

Egypt's economic future hinges on its ability to navigate these turbulent waters and implement its ambitious reform agenda. The IMF report serves as a reminder that the path to a private-sector-led resurgence will be long and arduous, requiring sustained commitment and decisive action.

(Chapter 26)

Iraq: Sensing the Potential: An Updated Look at Business Opportunities in Iraq

Iraq's potential as a lucrative market for investment remains undeniable, but the narrative has evolved. While significant opportunities exist, a nuanced understanding of the current economic landscape is crucial for investors. This chapter incorporates insights from the International Monetary Fund's (IMF) April 2024 Article IV Consultation report, providing a clearer picture of the challenges and opportunities in the Iraqi market.

Reconstruction and Rehabilitation: A Multi-Billion Dollar Opportunity

The commitment to rebuilding Iraq remains strong. The IMF report acknowledges the government's focus on stability and social cohesion, driving significant spending on public services and infrastructure. This creates a fertile ground for international businesses, particularly in construction, engineering, and related sectors. Think of it as tens of billions opportunity, ready for the taking, with projects spanning transportation, energy, and housing. The government's commitment to prioritizing high-impact projects, like the Grand Al-Faw Port and the Karbala Refinery, presents attractive opportunities.

Beyond Oil: Diversification and the Global Economy

While oil remains a key driver, potentially earning US$5 trillion in revenues between 2013-2035, Iraq is actively pursuing economic diversification. The IMF report emphasizes the need for structural reforms to unlock private sector-led growth. This opens doors for businesses in sectors like agriculture, manufacturing, and services.

Furthermore, global initiatives like China's Belt and Road Initiative (BRI) are poised to significantly impact the region, with planned investments in infrastructure, trade channels, and regulatory reform. Iraq, strategically located along the BRI's path, stands to benefit immensely from this global economic shift.

Navigating the Fiscal Landscape

The IMF report does highlight fiscal challenges, including a widening deficit and rising public debt, driven by a large public wage bill and declining oil prices. However, the government is actively pursuing solutions, including controlling expenditure, mobilizing non-oil revenues, and strengthening fiscal management through initiatives like the Integrated Financial Management System and the Treasury Single Account (TSA). This commitment to fiscal responsibility should reassure investors.

Favorable Investment Climate

Despite the challenges, Iraq offers a favorable investment climate. Competitive corporate and individual tax rates, along with attractive capital and investment requirements, make it an appealing destination for international businesses.

Opportunities Amidst Transition

The IMF report also highlights specific areas of opportunity for investors who understand the evolving landscape:

Digitalization: The push towards digital payments and financial inclusion creates opportunities for fintech companies and service providers.

Renewable Energy: Iraq's commitment to a decarbonization pathway and increasing reliance on renewable energy sources presents opportunities for investors in this sector.

Key Takeaways for Investors

Due Diligence: Thoroughly assess the fiscal risks and potential impact of oil price volatility on specific projects.

Partnerships: Collaborate with local partners to navigate the regulatory environment and leverage their expertise.

Long-Term Vision: Focus on projects that align with Iraq's long term development goals, such as economic diversification and private sector growth.

Conclusion: Sensing the Potential

The potential in Iraq is undeniable. Whether you are an international service provider, trader, manufacturer, construction contractor, or entrepreneur, the opportunities are vast. The IMF report provides valuable insights for navigating this dynamic market. With careful planning, strategic partnerships, and a long-term vision, investors can capitalize on Iraq's potential and contribute to its sustainable development.

The message remains clear: Are you able to sense the potential now?

Chapter (27)

Greece: A Strategic Economic and Investment Landscape Amid Recovery and Structural Transformation

Greece, having endured a decade of economic stagnation and crises, is now on a robust recovery trajectory. The economic landscape is marked by resilient growth, driven by strong tourism, bolstered investment, and continued fiscal reforms. However, as the IMF's 2023 Article IV consultation reveals, substantial risks remain, particularly from inflationary pressures, public debt, demographic challenges, and climate change. This chapter delves deeper into Greece's current economic situation, the trajectory of key indicators such as GDP growth, inflation, fiscal performance, and public debt, and the country's potential for investment across various sectors.

Steady Economic Growth and Inflation Pressures

Greece's economy demonstrated a strong rebound from the pandemic, with real GDP growing by 5.6% in 2022 and projected at 2.3% in 2023. This recovery has been notably robust, as the country's economic output surpassed pre-pandemic levels for the first time in over a decade. For 2024,

the IMF projects GDP growth to moderate slightly to 2.1%,
reflecting cooling momentum but still positioning Greece as
one of the stronger performers in the Eurozone.

Key drivers of this growth have included:

Tourism: A major contributor to the Greek economy,
tourism demand has significantly recovered post-pandemic,
exceeding 2019 levels. This sector alone remains a
cornerstone of Greece's economic recovery.

Investment: Boosted by Next Generation EU (NGEU)
funds, foreign direct investment (FDI), and structural
reforms, Greece has experienced a surge in investment,
particularly in sectors aligned with green and digital
transitions.

However, inflation remains a challenge, with headline
inflation decelerating from a high of 9.3% in 2022 to 4.2%
in 2023, and the IMF projects a further decline to 2.8% by
2024. Despite this, core inflation (excluding volatile food
and energy prices) remains sticky, hovering at 4.8% as of late
2023, primarily due to rising services costs and wage
pressures. The IMF's outlook suggests that while energy
prices will continue to normalize, wage increases in both the
public and private sectors will exert upward pressure on
inflation, complicating the ECB's inflation-targeting efforts.

Public Debt and Fiscal Sustainability

One of Greece's key achievements in recent years has been
the gradual reduction of its public debt-to-GDP ratio.
Following the pandemic, Greece's public debt peaked at

179.5% of GDP in 2022, but the strong post-pandemic recovery, high inflation, and fiscal consolidation efforts helped bring it down to 167.4% by 2023. The IMF forecasts a further decline to 158% by 2024.

This improvement in Greece's debt metrics is primarily due to the following factors:

Debt Structure: Greece's public debt is characterized by a favourable structure, with a large share held by official creditors, long maturities, and low fixed interest rates. This structure has shielded the country from the full effects of rising interest rates in the Eurozone.

Fiscal Consolidation: The government has implemented a growth-friendly fiscal consolidation, achieving a **primary surplus** (the fiscal balance excluding debt interest payments) of 1.1% of GDP in 2023, up from 0.1% in 2022. The IMF projects that Greece will maintain a primary surplus of 2.1% of GDP in 2024, underscoring the country's fiscal discipline.

However, challenges remain:

Structural Imbalances: Despite fiscal progress, Greece still faces structural imbalances, including low household savings and inadequate levels of investment, which weigh on medium-term growth prospects. The IMF also highlights the risks posed by demographic trends, particularly the decline in the working-age population, which is expected to decrease by 1% annually until 2030.

Fiscal Risks: The IMF suggests that while Greece's debt structure has helped reduce refinancing risks, higher public spending demands—especially on pensions and healthcare—could pressure future fiscal space, necessitating continued reforms.

External Sector Dynamics and Current Account Deficits

The current account of Greece has been a source of concern for several years. In 2022, Greece's current account deficit reached 10.7% of GDP, driven by high import prices and robust domestic demand. However, this deficit has been improving due to the reduction in energy prices and the strong performance of tourism. By mid-2023, the deficit narrowed to 7.1% of GDP, and the IMF forecasts a further reduction to 6.4% by year-end 2024.

Other notable external sector dynamics include:

FDI: Foreign Direct Investment (FDI) inflows into Greece, though relatively stable, remain modest compared to the Eurozone average, highlighting ongoing challenges in fully capitalizing on its economic potential. In absolute terms, FDI reached approximately €4.9 billion in 2022, marking a significant rebound driven by improvements in investor confidence and recovery momentum post-pandemic. However, inflows slightly tapered to an estimated €4.7 billion in 2023, underscoring the need for sustained efforts to enhance the business environment. The FDI-to-GDP ratio, at -2.1% in 2023, reflects these dynamics, with projections for 2024 anticipating a further dip to -2.9% as macroeconomic headwinds and structural inefficiencies persist.

While Greece has benefited from robust investment in specific sectors like tourism, energy, and shipping, broader diversification and increased scale remain critical. Structural impediments, such as regulatory complexity, the cost of doing business, and infrastructure gaps, continue to pose challenges to unlocking Greece's full FDI potential. Nevertheless, the government's focus on targeted reforms—such as the digitization of public services, streamlining of licensing processes, and promotion of strategic investments—provides a framework for improvement.

The implementation of Greece's National Recovery and Resilience Plan (NRRP), supported by EU funds, has the potential to attract greater FDI by prioritizing key areas such as renewable energy, technology, and infrastructure development. These investments align with Greece's long-term objectives of fostering sustainable and inclusive growth. Moreover, measures to enhance competitiveness and transparency, including tax incentives for green investments and fostering partnerships with international stakeholders, are expected to play a pivotal role in expanding FDI inflows.

Sustained efforts to address structural barriers and improve market conditions will be crucial in aligning Greece with its Eurozone peers in FDI performance, ultimately supporting its broader economic recovery and resilience strategy.

External Debt: Greece's external debt remains high, at 259% of GDP in 2023, but it continues to be supported by favourable financing terms. The external position remains weaker than expected, though the reduction in the current

account deficit may gradually improve Greece's external
balance.

Labor Market and Productivity Growth

The Greek labor market has shown notable improvements.
The unemployment rate has dropped from 12.4% in 2022 to
10.6% in 2023 and is expected to decline further to 9.2% in
2024. This marks a significant improvement over the past
decade, though youth unemployment remains stubbornly
high at 23.7%.

Key trends in Greece's labor market include:

Real Wage Growth: Real wages have increased in 2023,
supported by strong employment growth and a tightening
labor market. The unit labor cost remains competitive within
the Eurozone, contributing to Greece's improved
international competitiveness.

Productivity Challenges: Although Greece has seen a
recovery in labor productivity, it still lags behind the
Eurozone average, particularly in sectors reliant on digital
technologies and innovation. The IMF emphasizes that
further investment in skills development and digitalization
will be critical to raising productivity levels and addressing
labor shortages.

Financial System Resilience and Risks

Greece's financial system has displayed significant resilience,
largely due to its strengthened banking sector. The Non-
Performing Loan (NPL) ratio in the banking system fell

below 5% in 2023, marking a notable improvement since the sovereign debt crisis. The banks have benefitted from policy support, including the government-backed Hercules program, which has helped address NPLs.

However, the banking sector faces ongoing challenges:

Interest Rate Risks: As interest rates in the Eurozone remain elevated, Greece's banks face potential pressure on their profitability and capital adequacy. The IMF recommends strengthening liquidity management and implementing macroprudential policies, including activating a counter-cyclical capital buffer to safeguard against potential systemic shocks.

Real Estate Market: The real estate market has experienced a sharp recovery, with residential property prices increasing by more than 50% since the 2017 low. However, the IMF warns that house prices are overvalued by 6-29%, depending on the methodology used, indicating the risk of a market correction if financial conditions tighten further.

Structural Reforms: Green and Digital Transitions

The IMF highlights that Greece's medium-term growth will depend on its ability to address structural impediments and implement transformative reforms, particularly in green and digital sectors.

Green Transition: Greece has set ambitious climate goals, aiming to reduce its greenhouse gas emissions by 55% by 2030. The government has made progress in expanding renewable energy sources, but fossil fuels still dominate the energy mix, accounting for about 80% of energy consumption. Significant investments are needed to develop renewable energy infrastructure, improve energy efficiency, and modernize the electricity grid.

Digitalization: Greece has made strides in digital transformation, including the digitalization of government services, which has enhanced business productivity and tax compliance. However, the country lags behind in integrating digital technologies across sectors, especially among small and medium-sized enterprises (SMEs). Further efforts to improve digital skills, streamline regulations, and enhance the digital infrastructure will be key to raising Greece's productivity and competitiveness.

Key Takeaways for Investors

Investment in Green and Digital Sectors: Greece's strategic investment in renewable energy, digital infrastructure, and sustainable technologies offers significant growth potential. The ongoing reforms and the availability of EU funding make it an attractive destination for long-term investments in green and tech-driven sectors.

Fiscal and Debt Stability: Greece's debt trajectory is improving, but investors should monitor fiscal sustainability closely, particularly in light of the country's high public debt and ongoing structural imbalances. Fiscal reforms aimed at addressing tax evasion and increasing public investment will be critical in ensuring long-term fiscal stability.

Real Estate Caution: While the real estate market has shown strong recovery, overvaluation risks remain. Investors should approach the sector cautiously, especially given the potential for a market correction if interest rates continue to rise.

Labor Market and Productivity: With a growing labor force and improving real wage growth, Greece offers opportunities in sectors requiring skilled labor. However, addressing skill mismatches and increasing productivity through digitalization will be key to maintaining long-term competitiveness.

Conclusion: Greece's Path Forward

Greece's economic recovery and investment prospects are improving, bolstered by strong growth in tourism, EU-backed investments, and fiscal reforms. However, challenges remain in controlling inflation, managing public debt, and addressing structural weaknesses in the labor market and productivity. For investors

Chapter (28)

Qatar: A Rising Star in the Gulf

Qatar's successful hosting of the 2022 FIFA World Cup marked a pivotal moment in its decade-long journey towards economic diversification. This chapter draws upon the International Monetary Fund's (IMF) January 2024 Article IV Consultation report, explores the promising landscape of the Qatari market and the opportunities it presents for investors.

Beyond Gas: A Diversification Strategy in Action

While the hydrocarbon sector remains a cornerstone of the Qatari economy, the nation is actively pursuing diversification, as highlighted by the IMF report. Non-hydrocarbon growth, supported by substantial investments in public projects and the construction of the North Field LNG expansion project, is expected to drive economic expansion. Qatar's tourism sector, experiencing a boost from the World Cup legacy, is also poised for continued growth. The IMF projects medium-term growth to average around 5.5%, fueled by the North Field expansion and the implementation of the Third National Development Strategy (NDS3).

North Field Expansion: A Cornerstone of Growth

The North Field LNG expansion project, a massive undertaking, is set to significantly increase Qatar's LNG production capacity by 2028. This project presents a multi-billion-dollar opportunity for international businesses, particularly in construction, engineering, and related sectors. The expansion, coupled with increasing global demand for LNG, particularly from Asia and Europe, is projected to underpin Qatar's robust economic growth and solidify its position as a leading LNG exporter.

Navigating the Fiscal Landscape

The IMF report commends Qatar's commitment to fiscal prudence, evidenced by the significant fiscal and current account surpluses achieved in recent years. The report highlights the importance of maintaining this discipline while supporting economic transformation. Key recommendations include:

Sustained Fiscal Prudence: Adhering to a fiscal anchor based on the Permanent Income Hypothesis, ensuring intergenerational equity and resilience against external shocks.

Revenue Diversification: Introducing a broad-based VAT to modernize the tax system and broaden the revenue base.

Expenditure Optimization: Rationalizing the public wage bill, gradually phasing out remaining subsidies, and reorienting spending towards reforms that promote private sector-led growth.

A Stable and Secure Investment Climate

Qatar offers a stable and secure environment for foreign investors, underpinned by its strong macroeconomic fundamentals, prudent policies, and ongoing structural reforms. The IMF report acknowledges the progress made in enhancing labor market flexibility, improving the business environment, and promoting digital transformation. Key attractions for investors include:

Strong Financial Sector: Well-capitalized and liquid banks, coupled with initiatives to deepen domestic capital markets, provide a solid foundation for investment.

Attractive Business Environment: Ongoing efforts to streamline regulations, enhance administrative efficiency, and promote public-private partnerships create a favorable climate for businesses.

Strategic Location: Qatar's geographic position, coupled with its world-class infrastructure, makes it a strategic hub for regional and international trade.

Opportunities in a Transforming Economy

The IMF report identifies specific areas ripe for investment in Qatar:

Digitalization: Qatar's rapid progress in digital transformation, including the launch of a National Fintech

Strategy, presents opportunities for fintech companies, digital service providers, and technology innovators.

Renewable Energy: Qatar's commitment to climate action, guided by the National Environment and Climate Change Strategy, opens doors for investments in renewable energy, energy efficiency, and green finance.

Tourism and Hospitality: The tourism sector, benefiting from the World Cup legacy and ongoing initiatives to attract visitors, offers promising prospects for tourism operators, hospitality providers, and related businesses.

Human Capital Development: Investments in education, training, and skills development, aligned with the needs of a diversifying economy, are crucial for long-term growth and prosperity.

Key Takeaways for Investors

Strategic Alignment: Focus on projects aligned with NDS3 and QNV 2030, particularly those supporting economic diversification, private sector growth, and sustainability.

Partnership and Collaboration: Leverage local expertise and build strong partnerships to navigate the regulatory environment and maximize investment success.

Long-Term Perspective: Qatar's economic transformation is a long-term journey, requiring a patient and strategic approach from investors.

Qatar: A Rising Star in the Gulf

Qatar's economic outlook is bright, underpinned by its commitment to diversification, prudent policies, and a stable investment climate. The IMF report provides valuable insights for investors seeking to capitalize on the opportunities presented by this rising star in the Gulf. With careful planning, strategic partnerships, and a long-term vision, investors can contribute to Qatar's sustainable development and reap the rewards of its promising future.

Chapter (29)

Kuwait: Navigating Economic Winds Amidst Abundant Wealth

Kuwait, a nation blessed with abundant oil wealth, faces a critical juncture in its economic journey. While high oil prices have fuelled a robust recovery and impressive fiscal and external balances, the country must confront persistent structural challenges to secure a prosperous and sustainable future. This chapter post, drawing insights from the International Monetary Fund's (IMF) September 2023 Article IV Consultation report, explores the economic landscape of Kuwait, highlighting both its strengths and the pressing need for reforms.

Beyond the Black Gold: A Story of Resilience and Challenges

Kuwait's economy is deeply intertwined with oil, which dominates its GDP and exports. While non-oil GDP growth has demonstrated resilience, reaching an estimated 3.4 percent in 2021 and strengthening to 4.0 percent in 2022, the dominance of the oil sector underscores the urgency for economic diversification.

The IMF report projects continued non-oil growth, driven by domestic demand, but emphasizes that this growth must be accelerated and broadened to create sufficient opportunities for a young and growing Kuwaiti workforce.

Navigating Fiscal Currents: Balancing Short-Term Needs and Long-Term Sustainability

Kuwait's fiscal position has significantly improved, thanks to high oil revenues and expenditure restraint. The overall fiscal balance turned into a surplus of 6.5 percent of GDP in FY2021/22, with further improvement estimated for FY2022/23. However, the IMF report stresses that fiscal consolidation is crucial to reinforce long-term sustainability and intergenerational equity.

The report recommends a growth-friendly fiscal consolidation scenario, encompassing both non-oil revenue and expenditure measures, with a focus on:

Revenue Enhancement: Implementing a GCC-wide VAT and excises, expanding corporate income taxation, and enhancing revenue administration capacity.

Expenditure Rationalization: Curtailing the wage bill, gradually phasing out untargeted energy subsidies while enhancing social safety nets, and improving the efficiency of capital spending.

The Need for a New Compass: Embracing Structural Reforms

Kuwait faces deep-rooted structural challenges that hinder private sector-led growth and economic diversification. Key among these are:

Labor Market Segmentation: A large public sector offering high wages and job security has led to a concentration of Kuwaiti employment in this sector, leaving the private sector underdeveloped.

Declining Competitiveness: High public spending and wage growth have contributed to lower competitiveness, hindering private sector development.

Business Environment Bottlenecks: Despite efforts to improve the business environment, challenges remain, including land allocation procedures and restrictions on foreign ownership.

A comprehensive reform package

The IMF report underscores the need for a comprehensive reform package to address the above challenges, with a focus on:

Labor Market Reforms: Aligning public and private sector wage structures, promoting flexibility in hiring and firing workers, and adopting more flexible labor market policies for expatriates.

Social Safety Net Enhancement: Streamlining and enhancing the efficiency of social assistance programs to support workers during the transition.

Business Environment Improvements: Streamlining business procedures, relaxing restrictions on foreign ownership, improving land allocation mechanisms, and strengthening competition policy.

Investment in Human Capital: Enhancing education quality, expanding vocational training, and fostering research and innovation.

Key takeaways for investors

While these investment opportunities hold significant promise, investors need to carefully navigate the Kuwaiti investment landscape. Key considerations include:

Regulatory Environment: Understanding the regulatory framework and obtaining the necessary licenses and permits is crucial for successful investment.

Local Partnerships: Collaborating with local partners can provide valuable insights into the market, facilitate access to networks, and navigate cultural nuances.

Long-Term Vision: Investing in Kuwait requires a long-term perspective, as structural reforms and economic diversification take time to yield results.

By carefully considering these factors and aligning their investments with Kuwait's national development priorities, investors can contribute to the country's economic transformation while generating attractive returns.

Conclusion: Charting a Course for a Brighter Future

Kuwait stands at a crossroads. While its abundant oil wealth provides a cushion, the country must embrace comprehensive and well-sequenced reforms to navigate the changing global economic landscape. The IMF report offers valuable insights and recommendations for policymakers to chart a course towards a more diversified, dynamic, and sustainable economy, ensuring prosperity for current and future generations. The message is clear: Kuwait has the resources and potential to thrive in the post-oil era, but bold and decisive action is needed to unlock this potential.

Chapter (30)

Oman: Embracing a Future Beyond Oil

Oman's economic landscape is undergoing a remarkable transformation, driven by the ambitious goals outlined in Oman Vision 2040. This vision sets a clear path for the Sultanate to transition from an oil-dependent economy to a diversified and sustainable one, creating a wealth of opportunities for discerning investors. This chapter draws insights from the International Monetary Fund's (IMF) recent Article IV Consultation report, delves into the exciting developments shaping the Omani market and highlights the promising prospects that lie ahead.

Beyond Oil: A Steady Path to Diversification

While hydrocarbons have historically been the bedrock of Oman's economy, the nation is making significant strides in diversifying its economic base. Non-hydrocarbon growth accelerated to 2.1 percent in 2023, driven by a recovering agricultural and construction sector, as well as robust growth in services. This positive momentum is expected to continue, with the IMF projecting non-hydrocarbon growth to reach 4 percent over the medium term. This growth will be fueled by a confluence of factors, including global demand recovery, continued implementation of structural reforms, and a surge in private investment, particularly in non-hydrocarbon sectors.

Strategic Investments: Shaping a New Economy

Oman is strategically deploying its resources to cultivate a dynamic and diversified economy. Key initiatives driving this transformation include:

Harnessing Renewable Energy: Oman is capitalising on its abundant renewable resources, particularly solar and wind, to become a global leader in green hydrogen production. Energy Development Oman (EDO) has established Hydrom, a subsidiary dedicated to facilitating private sector-led investments in this burgeoning sector. With committed investments already exceeding $30 billion, green hydrogen is poised to become a cornerstone of Oman's future energy landscape.

Unlocking Tourism Potential: Oman boasts a wealth of natural beauty, from pristine coastlines and rugged mountains to captivating deserts and historical sites. Recognising the immense potential of its tourism sector, Oman is investing in expanding tourism infrastructure, enhancing flight connectivity, and improving the quality of tourism services. These efforts are aimed at attracting a larger share of global tourism, creating jobs, and boosting economic growth.

Building a Logistics Powerhouse: Oman's strategic location at the crossroads of major shipping routes and its ongoing investments in world-class logistics infrastructure position it to become a leading regional logistics hub. The government is actively streamlining customs procedures, enhancing the quality of trade-related infrastructure, and attracting private sector participation to unlock the full potential of this sector.

Leveraging Special Economic Zones (SEZs): Oman is strategically employing SEZs to attract foreign investment, foster industrial clusters, and promote technology transfer. The Public Authority for Special Economic Zones and Free Zones (OPAZ) is spearheading efforts to unify the regulatory framework of SEZs, further enhancing their attractiveness and competitiveness. These zones offer a range of incentives, including tax breaks, streamlined regulations, and access to a skilled workforce, making them attractive destinations for businesses looking to expand in the region.

Navigating the Fiscal Landscape

The IMF report commends Oman's commitment to fiscal discipline, evidenced by the remarkable turnaround from fiscal deficits to a surplus of 10.1 percent of GDP in 2022 and an estimated 5.5 percent in 2023. This achievement underscores the effectiveness of the government's fiscal consolidation efforts, which have included expenditure rationalisation, revenue diversification, and prudent debt management. Looking ahead, the government is actively pursuing further fiscal reforms to solidify these gains and enhance long-term fiscal sustainability. Key priorities include:

Tax Administration Reform: A comprehensive reform plan is underway to modernise tax administration, reduce the tax gap, and broaden the tax base. This includes exploring the potential introduction of a personal income tax, which would further diversify government revenue streams and enhance fiscal resilience.

Subsidy Reform: The government is committed to phasing out untargeted electricity and fuel subsidies, while simultaneously strengthening the social safety net to protect vulnerable households. This reform is crucial to promoting efficient resource allocation, reducing fiscal vulnerabilities, and creating a more sustainable energy sector.

Strengthening Fiscal Frameworks: Oman is taking steps to strengthen its medium-term fiscal framework (MTFF) and is exploring the adoption of a fiscal rule. These measures will enhance transparency, predictability, and accountability in fiscal policy, further bolstering investor confidence and ensuring intergenerational equity.

A Catalyst for Growth: A Favourable Investment Climate

Oman is actively fostering a welcoming investment climate, attracting foreign direct investment, and creating a fertile ground for businesses to thrive. Recent upgrades in sovereign credit ratings, to one notch below investment grade, reflect growing confidence in the country's economic prospects and its commitment to sound economic policies. Oman offers a compelling mix of attractive features for investors:

Business-Friendly Reforms: Oman has embarked on a series of business-friendly reforms aimed at streamlining regulations, reducing bureaucracy, and enhancing transparency. Reforms like the new Commercial Companies Law and the Foreign Capital Investment Law are simplifying processes for businesses, encouraging entrepreneurship, and attracting foreign investment. The government is committed to continuously improving the ease of doing business, making Oman an even more attractive destination for investors.

Enhanced Social Protection: The newly implemented social protection law is a cornerstone of Oman's commitment to building a more inclusive and equitable society. This comprehensive law provides a wide range of benefits, including universal child benefits, disability benefits, and senior citizen benefits, strengthening social safety nets and ensuring a basic level of support for all citizens. The law also promotes a more flexible labor market by harmonizing pension entitlements across public and private sectors, facilitating greater labor mobility.

Improved Governance: The Oman Investment Authority (OIA) is playing a key role in driving economic diversification and attracting foreign investment. Its Rawabet program is focused on enhancing governance, performance, and risk management within state-owned enterprises (SOEs). This program has introduced a robust Code of Governance for SOEs, implemented performance assessments, and established risk management frameworks, paving the way for increased private sector participation and a more competitive business environment. The OIA is also actively pursuing a strategic divestment program, opening up opportunities for private investors in sectors previously dominated by SOEs.

These initiatives, coupled with Oman's strategic location, abundant natural resources, and skilled workforce, create a compelling investment proposition for businesses seeking growth and expansion in a stable and promising market.

Key Takeaways for Investors

Oman's economic transformation under Oman Vision 2040 presents a unique opportunity for investors seeking growth and diversification in a stable and promising market. Here are key takeaways to consider:

Strategic Alignment: Align your investments with the strategic sectors outlined in Oman Vision 2040, such as renewable energy, tourism, logistics, manufacturing, and fisheries. These sectors offer significant growth potential and are supported by government initiatives and incentives.

Partnership Opportunities: Collaborate with local partners to leverage their expertise, navigate the regulatory environment, and gain access to local market knowledge and networks. Building strong partnerships can significantly enhance your chances of success in the Omani market.

Long-Term Perspective: Oman's economic transformation is a long-term endeavor. Adopt a patient and strategic approach to investment, focusing on building sustainable businesses that contribute to the country's long-term development goals.

By carefully considering these takeaways, investors can position themselves to capitalize on the exciting opportunities emerging in Oman's dynamic and evolving economy.

Conclusion: a story of constant growth and prosperity

Oman has made remarkable progress in strengthening its economy and is well-positioned for continued growth and prosperity. By sustaining its commitment to prudent fiscal management, pursuing ambitious structural reforms, and strengthening its monetary and financial frameworks, Oman can solidify its economic gains and achieve its Vision 2040 objectives.

Bahaa G. Arnouk

Chapter (31)

Jordan: A Beacon of Resilience in a Turbulent Region

Jordan's economy has demonstrated remarkable resilience in the face of a series of external shocks, maintaining macro-stability and achieving moderate economic growth. This chapter draws insights from the International Monetary Fund's (IMF) January 2024 report, provides a comprehensive overview of the challenges and opportunities present in the Jordanian market.

Weathering the Storm: A Story of Economic Resilience

Despite a challenging global and regional environment, marked by the COVID-19 pandemic, the war in Ukraine, and most recently the conflict in Gaza and Israel, Jordan has successfully navigated these turbulent times. Sound macroeconomic policies, coupled with significant international support, have enabled the country to maintain macro-stability and moderate economic growth, averaging 2-3 percent annually. Inflation, which had risen due to global commodity price shocks, has since fallen to low levels, thanks to adept monetary policy management by the Central Bank of Jordan (CBJ).

Addressing Challenges: A Focus on Jobs and Growth

While Jordan has weathered the storm effectively, challenges remain. Unemployment, particularly among youth and women, remains persistently high, and growth, while resilient, has not been sufficient to substantially reduce unemployment and raise incomes. Public debt, although stabilized, remains elevated. To address these challenges, the government, supported by a new four-year Extended Fund Facility (EFF) arrangement with the IMF, is focusing on accelerating structural reforms to achieve stronger, more inclusive growth and job creation.

Key Areas of Focus: A Roadmap for Reform

The IMF report highlights several key areas for reform and investment:

Fiscal Consolidation: The government is committed to continuing a gradual fiscal consolidation to place public debt on a steady downward path, while creating space for priority social spending and investment. This includes broadening the tax base, improving tax compliance, and enhancing public expenditure efficiency.

Financial Sector Resilience: The banking sector remains healthy and well-capitalized. The CBJ will continue to focus on preserving monetary and financial stability, safeguarding the exchange rate peg, and implementing the recommendations of the 2023 IMF-World Bank Financial System Stability Assessment.

Improving Efficiency of Public Utilities: The electricity and water sectors face significant financial challenges. The government is implementing reforms to improve their efficiency and financial viability, including tariff adjustments, cost-saving measures, and enhanced governance.

Accelerating Structural Reforms: To create a more dynamic private sector and foster job-rich growth, the government is accelerating structural reforms, guided by Jordan's Economic Modernization Vision. This includes improving the business environment, attracting higher levels of investment, introducing labor market reforms, and enhancing governance.

Opportunities for Investment: A Land of Potential

Despite the challenges, Jordan offers a range of opportunities for investors seeking to contribute to its sustainable development:

Tourism: With a rich history and cultural heritage, Jordan has significant potential for tourism development. The sector is expected to rebound as regional stability improves.

Information and Communication Technology (ICT): Jordan has a burgeoning ICT sector, with a skilled workforce and a supportive regulatory environment.

Renewable Energy: The country is committed to increasing the share of renewable energy in its energy mix, presenting opportunities for investment in solar and wind energy projects.

Infrastructure: Jordan has significant infrastructure needs, particularly in the water and transportation sectors, offering opportunities for investment in public-private partnerships.

Key Takeaways for Investors

Due Diligence: Thoroughly assess the political and economic risks and the potential impact of regional instability on specific projects.

Partnerships: Collaborate with local partners to navigate the regulatory environment and leverage their expertise.

Long-Term Vision: Focus on projects aligned with Jordan's Economic Modernization Vision, particularly those supporting economic diversification, private sector growth, and sustainability.

Conclusion: A Beacon of Hope

Jordan's commitment to economic reform and its resilience in the face of adversity make it a beacon of hope in a turbulent region. The IMF report provides valuable insights for navigating this dynamic market. With careful planning, strategic partnerships, and a long-term vision, investors can contribute to Jordan's sustainable development and capitalize on its potential for growth.

Chapter (32)

Cyprus: A Beacon of Resilience and Transformation in the Mediterranean

Cyprus's economy has consistently demonstrated resilience and adaptability in the face of numerous external shocks. This chapter draws upon insights from the International Monetary Fund (IMF) May 2024 Article IV Consultation report, offers a comprehensive analysis of the challenges and opportunities present in the Cypriot market.

Resilience Amid Challenges

Cyprus stands as a beacon of resilience in a turbulent global economic landscape, showcasing the power of strategic adaptation. Amidst the lingering effects of the pandemic, geopolitical shocks such as the war in Ukraine, and energy market volatility, the Cypriot economy has maintained momentum. Growth moderated to 2.5% in 2023, but this pace outperformed the euro area average, highlighting the island's economic dynamism. Cyprus growth catalysts are:

Sectoral Strengths: A recovery in tourism, the ascendancy of Information and communication technology (ICT) services, and robust financial activities are key drivers. Tourism arrivals rebounded to near-record levels in 2023, fueled by diversification into markets like Israel and the Middle East, offsetting losses from Russia.

Inflation Stability: Headline inflation declined to below 2% in 2023 due to falling energy prices and tight monetary policy. Core inflation, although stickier, was contained at 2.5%.

Labor Market Dynamics: Unemployment dropped to a historic low of 5.9%, underscoring the vitality of the job market. However, labor shortages in key sectors signal skill mismatches, creating both challenges and opportunities for reforms.

Despite a challenging external environment, the outlook remains positive, with growth projected at 2.6% in 2024 and an acceleration to 3% in the medium term. This stability hinges on robust FDI inflows, EU-funded Recovery and Resilience Plan (RRP) initiatives, and ongoing structural reforms.

Fiscal Landscape: Consolidation for a Sustainable Future

Cyprus's fiscal achievements stand out in Europe, with public debt declining sharply from its post-2013 crisis peak. In 2023, debt fell to 77.3% of GDP, cementing the nation's reputation for fiscal discipline. Primary surpluses, robust revenue generation, and strategic fiscal management are the cornerstones of this success.

Fiscal Challenges and Reform Opportunities:

Debt Reduction Priorities: Fiscal policy is centered on reducing public debt to below 60% of GDP by 2027, creating buffers against future shocks. Maintaining primary surpluses of around 4% of GDP is critical to achieving this goal.

Targeted Expenditure: Investments in infrastructure and green energy are prioritized, while temporary measures like electricity subsidies and VAT exemptions are being phased out. Controlling the public sector wage bill is a vital reform area.

Long-Term Pressures: Demographic trends and climate commitments are set to increase public spending by 2.5% of GDP by 2030. Careful fiscal planning to address these pressures while preserving Cyprus's social safety nets.

Financial Stability and Sectoral Resilience

Cyprus's banking and financial sector has emerged stronger, with capital and liquidity buffers exceeding regulatory requirements. However, challenges remain, particularly in addressing legacy non-performing loans (NPLs) and managing real estate-related risks. Key insights are:

Banking Sector Health: Cyprus's banks are well-positioned to withstand macroeconomic shocks, with stress tests indicating resilience. Loan renegotiations have increased, reflecting proactive risk management.

Real Estate Vigilance: The property market remains buoyant, driven by foreign demand, yet systemic risks persist. With two-thirds of loans secured by real estate, ongoing regulatory vigilance is essential.

Legacy NPL Resolution: Cyprus's ambitious climate goals present a dual challenge and opportunity. The nation seeks to achieve climate neutrality by 2050, with interim goals including a 32% reduction in non-EU Emissions Trading System (ETS) sector emissions by 2030. This transition offers fertile ground for investors in green technology, renewable energy, and sustainable infrastructure. Investments highlights are:

Renewable Energy: Expanding solar, wind, and energy storage capacities is central to Cyprus's energy strategy. The delayed LNG terminal, expected to be operational by 2025, will further enhance energy diversification.

Green Taxation and Carbon Pricing: The IMF supports broadening the carbon tax scope to all non-ETS sectors, coupled with targeted support for vulnerable households. This approach balances fiscal goals with equity concerns.

Adaptation Measures: With rising temperatures and sea levels, investments in climate resilience, such as coastal protection and water resource management, are critical.

Regulatory and Tax Framework: A Strategic Reset

Cyprus is aligning its regulatory environment with international best practices, focusing on anti-money laundering (AML) and combating financing of terrorism (CFT). A single supervisory framework for administrative services and enhanced oversight of the real estate sector are key priorities.

Tax System Overhaul

The ongoing review of Cyprus's tax system aims to modernize it for the digital age while ensuring alignment with the EU's tax directives. Green taxation and a fairer income tax regime are at the forefront of reforms.

Taxation and Revenue Enhancements

Green taxation, aligned with climate objectives, is a pivotal reform. Coupled with the EU's 15% minimum corporate income tax for multinationals, Cyprus is overhauling its tax regime to ensure fairness, efficiency, and sustainability. VAT system optimization and enhanced compliance mechanisms further boost revenue potential.

Investment Climate: Unlocking Cyprus's Potential

Cyprus's investment appeal lies in its strategic location as a gateway between Europe, the Middle East, and Africa, bolstered by EU membership, a skilled workforce, and a business-friendly regulatory framework. The IMF 2024 Article IV Consultation highlights several sectoral opportunities where the island nation excels, while also identifying areas for reform and innovation to enhance its attractiveness to global investors.

Information and Communication Technology (ICT): Building a Regional Tech Hub

Cyprus is rapidly establishing itself as a premier destination for ICT investments. The government's focus on digital transformation is supported by significant advancements in infrastructure, including nationwide 5G coverage and an expanding fiber-optic network. Key initiatives aim to position Cyprus as a leader in artificial intelligence (AI), blockchain, and cybersecurity.

Supportive Policy Environment: National digital strategies prioritize innovation, data protection, and e-government services. The Recovery and Resilience Plan (RRP) includes €282 million allocated for digital transformation projects, signaling robust state support for ICT growth.

Emerging Opportunities: Growth in fintech, cybersecurity, and cloud computing services is attracting global companies. The island's integration into the EU's Digital Single Market further enhances its potential as a regional ICT hub.

Talent Development: Addressing skill shortages remains a priority, with reforms in education to promote STEM fields and targeted initiatives to upskill workers in emerging technologies.

Tourism and Real Estate: A Pillar of Economic Growth

Tourism remains a cornerstone of Cyprus's economy, with a remarkable post-pandemic recovery fueled by a strategic pivot to new markets. The country's idyllic Mediterranean setting, coupled with its rich cultural heritage, makes it a perennial favorite among tourists and real estate investors alike.

Tourism Recovery and Diversification: While traditional markets such as Russia faced disruptions, Cyprus successfully attracted visitors from the Middle East, Israel, and Europe. New tourism initiatives emphasize sustainable travel, eco-tourism, and the promotion of lesser-known regions.

Real Estate Investments: The property market is buoyed by demand from foreign buyers, particularly for high-end residences and commercial properties. Non-EU investors account for a significant portion of this activity, with attractive visa and residency schemes as key incentives.

Infrastructure Development: The government has prioritized investment in transport, urban regeneration, and smart city projects, further boosting the appeal of the real estate sector.

Professional Services: A Thriving Sector with Global Reach

Cyprus's robust legal, accounting, and financial services ecosystem is a testament to its adaptability and alignment with international standards. These services continue to attract multinational corporations and high-net-worth individuals.

Legal and Accounting Expertise: The island is a preferred jurisdiction for corporate structuring, tax planning, and cross-border legal advisory services, thanks to its competitive tax regime and compliance with EU regulations.

Financial Services: A diversified banking sector, coupled with regulatory alignment with the EU and OECD standards, strengthens Cyprus's reputation as a financial hub.

Emerging trends include the growth of green finance and ESG-aligned investment opportunities.

AML/CFT Improvements: Strengthened anti-money laundering frameworks, as recognized by the IMF, enhance Cyprus's standing as a credible and secure destination for professional services.

Addressing Challenges: Innovation and Reform

While Cyprus has made impressive strides in economic resilience and investment attractiveness, several challenges remain that necessitate targeted interventions and innovative strategies to sustain growth and competitiveness. These include addressing labor market dynamics, streamlining governance and bureaucracy, and mitigating geopolitical and external risks.

Labor Market Pressures: Bridging Gaps and Building Skills

The tight labor market, with unemployment at historic lows, underscores Cyprus's economic vitality but also reveals critical inefficiencies. A pronounced mismatch between available jobs and workforce skills is evident, particularly in high-demand sectors such as ICT, tourism, and healthcare.

Education System Overhaul

Aligning educational outcomes with labor market needs is essential. The government is focusing on modernizing curricula to include more digital and technical skills, increasing STEM graduates, and promoting vocational training.

Digital Readiness: Investment in digital education and infrastructure aims to prepare the younger workforce for technology-driven industries.

Upskilling Initiatives: Programs targeting adult workers in declining industries will help transition them into growing sectors like renewable energy and digital services.

Labor Force Expansion

The labor shortages in sectors like tourism and construction necessitate strategic policies to attract foreign talent while addressing underutilized segments of the domestic workforce.

Gender and Youth Participation: Measures to increase participation rates among women and young people, including childcare support and career counseling, are critical.

Immigration Reforms: Streamlined procedures for work permits, particularly for high-skilled workers, aim to attract global talent.

Activation Policies: Stricter requirements for job seekers, coupled with incentives for private-sector job creation, are designed to reduce structural unemployment and enhance labor force productivity.

Governance and Bureaucratic Efficiency: Creating a Business-Friendly Environment

Cyprus has made progress in governance reforms, but inefficiencies in bureaucracy and judicial processes continue to deter investment. Addressing these systemic issues is critical to fostering a more transparent and predictable business environment.

Judicial System Enhancements:

Ongoing reforms aim to reduce case backlogs and accelerate dispute resolution.

Digitization of Courts: Investments in e-justice platforms and digital case management systems are expected to significantly reduce delays and increase transparency.

Specialized Courts: The establishment of commercial courts focuses on expediting business-related disputes, improving confidence among investors.

Regulatory Streamlining: Simplifying business processes is a priority to reduce administrative burdens on companies.

One-Stop-Shop Services: Consolidated service centers for business registration and compliance are being enhanced to minimize red tape.

Regulatory Predictability: Efforts to harmonize regional and federal regulatory frameworks aim to provide clarity and stability to investors.

Transparency and Anti-Corruption: Strengthened anti-corruption frameworks and improved oversight mechanisms are integral to boosting public trust and international credibility.

AML/CFT Improvements: Implementation of the MONEYVAL recommendations continues, with a focus on addressing vulnerabilities in the real estate sector and administrative services.

Geopolitical and External Risks: Building Resilience and Diversification

As a small open economy, Cyprus remains highly vulnerable to external shocks, particularly those affecting its key sectors like tourism and professional services. Proactive measures to diversify economic reliance and build resilience are essential.

Tourism Diversification: While the rebound in tourism has been robust, over-reliance on specific markets, such as the EU and Israel, leaves Cyprus exposed to geopolitical tensions and economic slowdowns in these regions.

Expanding Source Markets: Strategic marketing efforts are targeting Asia and the Americas to attract a more diverse pool of tourists.

Sustainable Tourism Development: Investments in eco-tourism and off-season travel options aim to stabilize revenue streams.

Trade and Investment Diversification: Cyprus's export profile, heavily skewed towards services, is being balanced with initiatives to boost manufacturing and high-value goods production.

Strategic Sectors: Renewable energy and pharmaceuticals are being prioritized for export expansion.

Regional Trade Alliances: Strengthening ties with non-EU partners in the Middle East and Africa is a focus area to mitigate regional geopolitical risks.

Climate and Energy Security: Cyprus is vulnerable to climate-related risks, including rising sea levels and extreme weather, which threaten infrastructure and economic stability.

Renewable Energy Investments: Accelerating the deployment of solar, wind, and energy storage systems reduces reliance on volatile energy imports.

Climate Adaptation Strategies: Policies to safeguard coastal areas and manage water resources are being implemented to protect critical assets.

Cyprus recognizes that overcoming these challenges requires bold reforms and sustained innovation. By addressing labor market inefficiencies, streamlining governance, and diversifying economic dependencies, the nation is positioning itself as a resilient and adaptive economy. These efforts are critical not only for mitigating risks but also for unlocking new growth opportunities in an increasingly competitive global landscape.

Key Messages for Investors

Cyprus presents a compelling case for investment, blending resilience with significant growth potential. Its transition toward a greener and more digital economy, backed by EU funding and national reforms, creates opportunities across multiple sectors.

Sectoral Opportunities: ICT, green energy, tourism, and professional services are poised for growth, underpinned by government and EU support.

Strategic Alignments: Investors aligning with Cyprus's RRP goals and climate transition agenda will find favorable policies and incentives.

Local Partnerships: Collaborating with Cypriot entities can help navigate regulatory complexities and unlock market-specific insights.

Sustainability and Innovation: Green finance and digital solutions are integral to Cyprus's long-term strategy, offering investors avenues to contribute to and benefit from sustainable development.

By embracing innovation, fostering resilience, and leveraging its strategic location, Cyprus is well-positioned to attract global investors and solidify its status as a hub for sustainable growth and innovation.

Conclusion: Seizing the Momentum

Cyprus's commitment to economic transformation, supported by sound macroeconomic policies and a stable investment climate, presents a compelling opportunity for investors seeking growth and diversification. The IMF report provides valuable insights for navigating this dynamic market. With careful planning, strategic partnerships, and a long-term vision, investors can capitalize on Cyprus's potential and contribute to its sustainable development.

The message is clear: Are you ready to seize the momentum in Cyprus?

Bahaa G. Arnouk

References

- IMF Country Report No. 24/232 on United States of America
- IMF Country Report No. 24/258 on China
- IMF Country Report No. 24/229 on Germany
- IMF Country Report No. 24/118 on Japan
- IMF Country Report No. 23/426 on India
- IMF Country Report No. 24/203 on United Kingdom
- IMF Country Report No. 24/216 on France
- IMF Country Report No. 24/240 on Italy
- IMF Country Report No. 24/128 on Canada
- IMF Country Report No. 24/209 on Brazil
- IMF Country Report No. 23/369 on South Korea
- IMF Country Report No. 24/317 on Mexico
- IMF Country Report No. 24/11 on Australia
- IMF Country Report No. 24/152 on Spain
- IMF Country Report No. 24/270 on Indonesia
- IMF Country Report No. 24/312 on Turkey
- IMF Country Report No. 24/85 on Netherlands
- IMF Country Report No. 24/280 on Saudi Arabia
- IMF Country Report No. 24/179 on Switzerland
- IMF Country Report No. 24/167 on Argentina
- IMF Country Report No. 23/223 on UAE
- IMF Country Report No. 24/107 on Austria
- IMF Country Report No. 24/255 on Singapore

Global Economy Shifting Currents: Unveiling Global
Economic Realities and Investment Frontiers

- IMF Country Report No. 24/73 on Malaysia
- IMF Country Report No. 24/274 on Egypt
- IMF Country Report No. 24/128 on Iraq
- IMF Country Report No. 24/23 on Greece
- IMF Country Report No. 24/43 on Qatar
- IMF Country Report No. 23/331 on Kuwait
- IMF Country Report No. 24/31 on Oman
- IMF Country Report No. 24/10 on Jordan
- IMF Country Report No. 24/137 on Cyprus